FOUNDATIONAL
LEADERSHIP

GROWTH DOESN'T START AT THE TOP

FOUNDATIONAL LEADERSHIP

ROBERT L. GRIGGS

Advantage | Books

Published by Advantage, Charleston, South Carolina.
Member of Advantage Media.

ADVANTAGE is a registered trademark, and the Advantage colophon is a trademark of Advantage Media Group, Inc.

Printed in the United States of America.

10 9 8 7 6 5 4 3 2 1

ISBN: 978-1-64225-337-5 (Hardcover)
ISBN: 978-1-64225-440-2 (eBook)

LCCN: 2022917371

Book design by Wesley Strickland.

This publication is designed to provide accurate and authoritative information in regard to the subject matter covered. It is sold with the understanding that the publisher is not engaged in rendering legal, accounting, or other professional services. If legal advice or other expert assistance is required, the services of a competent professional person should be sought.

Advantage Media helps busy entrepreneurs, CEOs, and leaders write and publish a book to grow their business and become the authority in their field. Advantage authors comprise an exclusive community of industry professionals, idea-makers, and thought leaders. Do you have a book idea or manuscript for consideration? We would love to hear from you at **AdvantageMedia.com**.

CONTENTS

FOREWORD

I like it when someone who has the desire to write a book actually does. I like reading about a person's point of view and the lessons one has learned about life, especially business.

It is fascinating to learn the various steps people go through to attain a goal or reach success. We all need those helpful hints, whether we are trying to get ahead or maybe thinking about starting a business or a new career.

Robert Griggs, in his storytelling format, has done just that in his new book, *Foundational Leadership: Growth Doesn't Start at the Top*! The book takes us from the very start of his career to the present and explains the challenges he has overcome and the opportunities he has attained with others.

There are a lot of business books on the market today, but Robert's personal approach makes it feel that he is talking directly to you. And he is sharing his personal and professional growth as his business goes through its growth cycles. No long-term success can be achieved without great leadership and Robert points out the importance of "collective buy-in," which empowers his leadership team and associates.

One of his interesting strategies has to do with expecting the unexpected. He believes that opportunities come when you are least prepared to handle them, and that timing is always off. I never looked at opportunities from that perspective and he may be right.

At the core of his message on leadership and growth, "relationship building" is the most consistent focus. Know a person enough to be open around the tasks to be accomplished. Commit to one another and strive to be the best. His culture centers around openness and transparency. He teaches new ways to teach people business and people see things from a different perspective. He promotes opening the books and showing people how they make a difference and can grow their livelihood as well.

When it comes to strategic thinking well, I let you be the judge on whether this unfolds a master plan or a result of unexpected opportunities. Regardless, he has, as have his associates, created an incredible company with high values and high results. They have built a platform for people to succeed and benefit from running an outrageously successful company.

Upon completion of reading this book, I was glad I did. There were takeaways after every chapter that are applicable right now. There were golden nuggets spread across each chapter. They were about the real growth of a person, associates, customers, and of a company.

Don't miss out on the opportunity to learn through the lives of others. This is a journey of growth.

Jack Stack
CEO, SRC Holdings Corporation,
author of *The Great Game of Business*

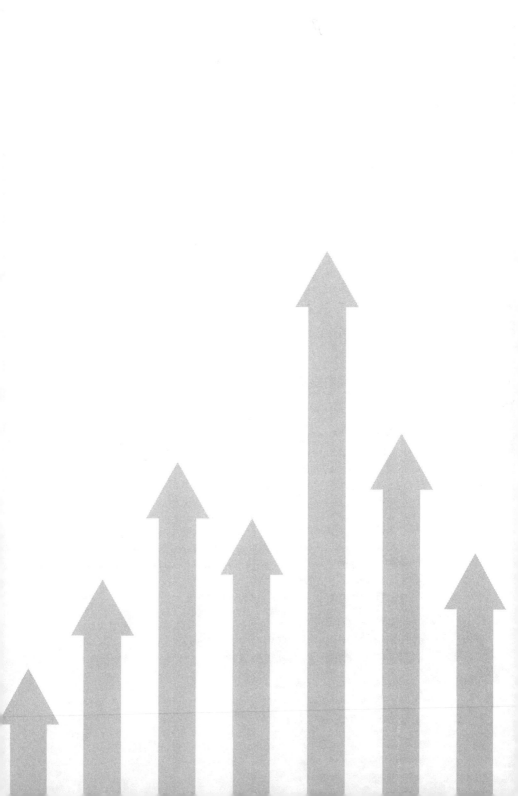

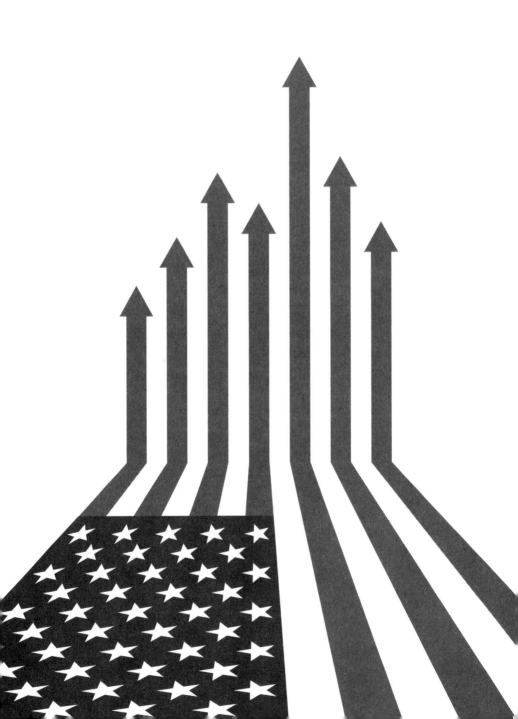

INTRODUCTION

You should write a book. These are five words I have heard with growing frequency over the past decade of my life. It started with the occasional friend making the lighthearted suggestion but soon grew into a choir of voices asking me to bring my story and the history of Trinity Products to words on a page. This got the wheels turning in my mind.

Around five years ago, I was on a plane traveling across the United States when I began to write my story and the history of my company. As I did, I became more engrossed in the process. Before I knew it, I had pages of notes typed up in a Word document and knew I had something.

Unfortunately, a few days later disaster struck. Someone from my IT department kindly offered to upgrade my laptop. And without giving it much thought, I traded my old one, and they wiped it clean. In the process, I failed to save all the work I had started on this book. And before I knew it, those twenty thousand words were a mere memory. This left me to wonder if the idea of writing a book would remain an idea forever. But despite this setback, I knew this was something I needed to do.

In July 2020, I was chatting with a venture capital guy from California when he made this remark: "You make business sound so simple. Have we just made it too hard?"

I paused and then nodded yes. "Business is simple," I told him, "but it's just hard to execute day after day—like everything else in life."

That was when he added his voice to the choir with those five key words: "You should write a book!"

At that point I knew I needed to do something and resolved to start the process again. I called my friend Jack Stack, whom I reference several times in this book and who is someone who served as the inspiration for the way Trinity conducts business today. We talked for half an hour, and he addressed the need to help leaders in any position—managers, entrepreneurs, and business owners—to flourish.

After I hung up the phone, I started writing.

There are some days I swear it feels like Big Brother is listening to you. A few days after this conversation, I received a call from Advantage|Forbesbooks, and their representative introduced himself with a proposal to write a book. As he spoke, *Twilight Zone* music started to play in my head, and as a sales guy, I immediately assumed some electronic device had heard me mention writing a book on one of my office computers, and some algorithm had prompted them to give me a call.

Much to my relief, when I asked the representative, he assured me that had not been the case. This left me to shrug in amazement at how the universe works. As we spoke for more than an hour, I shared a rough outline of the story I am about to unpack in the coming pages. I told him about how I got started in sales and how several twists and turns directed me to start my own business. I shared several of the key principles that helped us succeed for over forty years.

And as I prepare to share these with you, the reader, I can tell you there is no magic sauce contained in the following pages (I guess this doesn't make me much of a salesperson!). But I can offer you some hope for your journey. I can share how I took a start-up company to over $300 million in organic, nonacquisitional annual sales.

The great news is my story is not complicated. As I tell any business leader I encounter, you can do great things if you just master the fundamentals. It starts with showing up each day with a desire to have fun, tell the truth, work hard and smart, and, most important, lead from the bottom. The folks at the bottom of the organizational pyramid are your foundation and those you must win over each day. They are the heart and soul of your company. If they succeed, you succeed. If they fail, you fail. You will hear me repeat this old concept repeatedly in the coming pages: the more you give, the more you receive. Because I believe this with all my heart, I have determined to be the greatest giver I can be, and I challenge you to do the same.

> **As I tell any business leader I encounter, you can do great things if you just master the fundamentals.**

Instead of being a constant taskmaster who urges troops into battle each day, become a servant of others and seek to elevate them in place of yourself. Remember, your boss is always the customer, and your best assets are your employees.

After implementing the same basic principles for decades, my Trinity leadership team and I are convinced we could enter any arena of business today and sell any product using the systems and structures we have and be enormously successful. These concepts are that good.

I mention this because you might know a bit about my history in the steel industry and be tempted to think, "Well, these ideas Robert has might work for his organization, but there is no way they will work in a different environment." I can assure you they will, because they are universal in how your employees and customers want to be served.

Leading an organization, at any level, is hard work. But there are steps you can take that will make you a stronger leader and create an environment where your team wants to show up to work.

There is no magic formula. The principles I outline are simple, and the toughest part is executing them every single day. Are you ready? Do you have the desire to take this journey? If so, it's time to take the leap.

Takeaways

➡ Always back up your work!

➡ Think of some ways you can focus on the foundation of your org chart to help build relationships.

➡ Your boss is your customer—how can you better serve your customers and make their lives easier?

➡ The more you give, the more you receive.

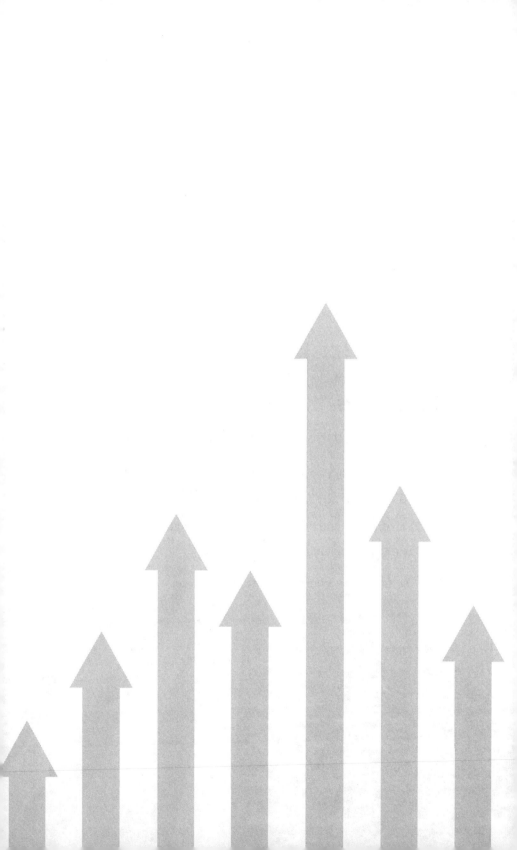

CHAPTER 1

TAKE THE LEAP

The day I got cheated out of a $5,000 commission check was a turning point in my life.

It was 1978, and I was making around $700 a month, plus commission, selling to end users and pipe distributers. The small steel pipe company I worked for was based out of Denver, and one of our major clients was Valley Steel—the king of the pipe universe. While other companies such as ours were getting by with only a couple of million in annual sales, Valley Steel dominated the industry, selling $200 million of pipe at a time when prime steel sold for $400 a ton (about a fifth of what that same product costs today).

Because they were the titans of our industry, I worked hard to establish strong sales connections. Fortunately, my sales manager, Sal, used to work for them and knew all the key players. The introductions he made soon paid off, and within a few months I sold them five thousand feet of forty-eight-inch-by-five-hundred-inch surplus pipe off the Alaskan Pipeline. Because I made a dollar-per-foot commission, this sale looked like my first big payday.

With this purchase order finalizing just a few months before Christmas, I looked forward to a prosperous holiday season. A few days before December 25, I received an envelope in the mail from our company and tore it open with excitement, grateful I had finally struck it big! To my dismay, the only thing inside was a fifty-dollar Christmas bonus check from my company. Normally I would have been grateful, but not today.

I called up the owner of my company in Denver and asked him about the commission check. He responded by telling me Valley Steel had not paid him, and there was nothing he could do. I couldn't believe what I heard, and something about that didn't ring true. I knew the guys at Valley Steel, and they were good people. Something was wrong.

Being young and naive I called up Harold Mayberry, the chief financial officer (CFO) of Valley Steel, and asked, "Hey, my boss says you haven't paid us. Is that true?"

His response stunned me. "Ask your boss how much your company owes *us*."

I hung up the phone, angry and feeling cheated. The owner of my company I had just spoken with not thirty minutes before knew all about this arrangement all along. He understood that any money we made on the sale of steel would be used to pay down his company's debt and would not find its way to me in the foreseeable future.

Later that afternoon, I walked into Sal's office, told him what happened, and announced I was going to quit. That was when Sal threw out an interesting proposition.

"Why don't we both quit and start our own company?" he asked.

Something about Sal's question rang true. A few days later I said goodbye for good to working for someone else, and with $15,000 we launched Trinity Products.

I Always Knew I Would Start My Own Business

But as with any great leap, there are often a series of life events that make that step appealing. For me, my entrepreneurial journey began in my teenage years.

Starting my own business was something I had always wanted to do. The how, where, or why were never clear, but I knew this was the path for me. It was only a matter of time before it happened, and the mistreatment I experienced gave me the perfect excuse to chart a new course.

This thought of being my own boss was probably a mixture of circumstance, willpower, and genetics. Something inside told me I wanted more, but I can also see how my upbringing shaped my entrepreneurial personality.

I grew up in an army family and traveled all over the world till the seventh grade, when we moved back to my dad's hometown of Charleston, Missouri. This was a community of haves and have-nots. There were the uber wealthy and those living paycheck to paycheck. That said, there was little talk about which of these two groups you were in. Even though my family landed in the have-not category, my dad made sure we focused on the one thing in life we could control—work ethic. He instilled in me the desire to outwork everyone around, and this mindset served me well even before I became my own boss.

A pivotal moment occurred in 1970 when my mother passed away from a heart attack. With my older sister already off to college, I was left alone in a house with just my dad. This painful experience forced me to grow up at a young age and made me take responsibility for my needs and wants.

Part of taking responsibility involved getting a job. In 1969, at age fifteen, I met a local farmer named Ed Marshall, who owned a farm of over ten thousand acres. He hired me, and I worked with him almost every summer until my senior year in college. Mr. Marshall trusted me and handed me more and more responsibilities.

At sixteen, I managed seven of his hired hands. Most were young girls who would sit on the front of the tractor and spray the fields for weeds as I drove. But this small step into leadership increased my confidence, and Mr. Marshall's passion motivated me to succeed. "Robert, think about how much land we could farm if we only ran the tractors all night long!" he would tell me.

There was a healthy sense of mutual respect. I wanted to be like him, and he could see I was good at my job and eager to succeed. We became friends.

While I did not see it then, every experience I gained during this season prepared me for the day I would start my company. It toughened me up and gave me the inner confidence I needed to succeed.

Growing Pains

In the early days of Trinity, Sal and I formed a strong partnership. He was a tough, conservative, and principled business owner. There was no way he was going to let an outside situation end our business.

Because he was tough, we had our share of healthy disagreements. I would push him on the need to expand, and he would urge me to play it safe. I had to beg him to purchase a fax machine, and every new area of expansion felt like a battle. We had two different mindsets that were incompatible for the long haul. He wanted to collect a stable paycheck, and I wanted to grow and improve every day.

Due to his gruff "I'm the boss" nature, I often felt I was in a place of damage control with the employees in our company, trying to smooth over tough conversations. There was always some form of drama taking place. As our company expanded and we hired more people, this grew more tiresome, and one situation became the final straw.

At this point in our company's history, we were in only the structural- and used-pipe business. It wasn't glamorous, but we cut and welded pipe and built a strong customer base.

Eventually, we made rolled-and-welded pipe. This involved taking plate cut to the correct length and rolling it into a pipe can. Then we would weld these together to make new pipe. This was a natural progression for our business, because we could now make any size outside diameter (OD) or thickness and expand what we offered customers. This took us into the fabrication of signs and diversified our business.

While traveling to a plate mill in the south (Tuscaloosa Steel), I saw heavy-gauge forty-eight-inch-by-one-inch coils all thrown into a pile. "What are those?" I asked.

The manager responded that they were "hot box coils" and considered scrap because they had cooled below pliability and couldn't be rolled.

My eyes lit up when I saw this, because it seemed like a great opportunity just waiting to be brought to market. (I've found these kinds of opportunities are always out there if you keep your eyes open and have some imagination.)

This pointed me back to my friends at Valley Steel. They had a fifty-year-old cobble leveler that could level up to four-inch plates. They were used to level cobble plates that were rejected because they were not flat after they cooled.

This led me to an important question: *How do we get the coils pulled and cut to have the plates leveled?* After giving it some thought, I worked out a deal with a company to pull the coils and torch them into twenty-foot lengths. Then Valley Steel would do the job of leveling. This meant I could buy coils of steel for just a few cents, have them cut and leveled, and turn a 25 percent profit for a new market. It seemed like a match made in heaven!

This went well at first, but after my third round of purchases, Valley Steel said the leveler was broken and would take $1,000 to repair. I offered to cover the costs myself, but they were not interested. There was a rumor that they were close to going out of business—one I found hard to believe.

I asked if I could buy it from them, and they agreed to sell it for $5,000. Here was the problem. When I took this purchase idea to Sal, he wasn't interested. From his viewpoint, it was too much money and too much risk. Finally, after much back-and-forth, he consented, but only on the condition that I sold another one of our pieces of equipment to cover the costs.

We selected our pipe-cleaning machine, and that weekend I stood in front of our new fax machine and sent out sales flyers to every used-pipe company in America. The pipe-cleaning machine sold that weekend—catching Sal a bit off guard. He had hoped this caveat would discourage me from moving forward, and when it sold that fast, he had no interest in this new purchase, which he did not understand or want. I said that was no problem and bought it anyway. When he asked where I was going to put the leveler, I told him I would place it on my half of the lease we had signed.

Because we were fifty-fifty partners, there was little he could do, and this breakdown in communication spelled the end of our business partnership. It was in the summer of 1992. Sal and I had been in business together for thirteen years, but now it was obvious our paths were heading in different directions. For the next six months, I was at the yard every morning at 4:30 a.m., leveling plate. My wife, Shelly, would come by with the boys and bring us dinner, and I would return to the house after dark. There were a lot of long days, flush with the excitement of progress and cash.

By Christmas, everyone could see we had had an exceptional year, and I pitched a Christmas party for our company employees to celebrate. Sal opted not to join. That night, after a few beers, the guys gave me an ultimatum. Buy Sal out and end the awkward drama, or they were going to quit.

I realized I had to do something. On Monday, I told Sal what happened and said one of us had to leave. To Sal's credit, he was gracious and established a fair price of $125,000, and I bought out his share of the company. While this change was painful in the moment, it proved to be worth it in the end. At the time, we sold $2.2 million in sales. In ten years after Sal's departure, I would sell the leveler and coil-pulling device for $250,000—more than covering the cost of his buyout.

Despite our differences, I often say Sal is the reason I made it to where I am today. Without him, I am sure I would have made a major mess of our company in the early days and spent us into the ground. He was a needed voice in my life that kept me on track, and we concluded our partnership on a positive note.

Everyone Is an Entrepreneur

While I cannot deny I have a unique knack for sales and entrepreneurship, I firmly believe everyone is an entrepreneur at heart. This is good news if you live in America.

As someone who has traveled the globe, I am grateful for the unique blessings Americans enjoy. In the United States, everyone has the chance to be an entrepreneur. You just need to find something you like to do and that others need. Hopefully you have the passion for it, but this is not a prerequisite. So long as you stick with it and adapt with change, you can build a prosperous company. This might come through starting your own business, but it might come through teaming up with someone else who shares your entrepreneurial values.

> In the United States, everyone has the chance to be an entrepreneur. You just need to find something you like to do and that others need.

One of the real gifts of America is the belief that any person can be president. Yes, we still have injustice and barriers that obstruct some from climbing up the ladder as quickly as others, but the dream is still possible. For citizens of many other countries, this is not the case. You might have a division between the wealthy and those in poverty. Or there might be a healthy middle class but little room for them to grow into the next level.

Whenever someone complains to me that they do not have enough opportunity, I think back to my story. I wasn't exactly born with a silver spoon in my mouth and faced my share of challenges. Instead of having a parent who paid my way through college, I took a job as a school bus driver and worked part time at a clothing store. This was hard, but it was good. It taught me that if I put my head down and worked hard, I could make something of myself.

My Tips for Young Entrepreneurs

The longer I have been an entrepreneur, the less I can define it. There are so many intangibles.

I know what it means to be a great leader and to be someone others want to follow. I am disciplined, treat people right, and have high expectations for those in my organization. One statement I often make to my team is that "you are either the guy who throws the can on the ground, walks by it, or picks it up." I want to work with people who care enough to pick it up.

Entrepreneurship is different. There are so many intangibles that make up great entrepreneurs. And while I'm afraid I cannot provide a one-two-three-step formula that will see you replicate the success of great entrepreneurs, I do have some tips.

TIP 1: MEASURE YOUR GOALS

Anything worth doing is worth measuring. This is a phrase I often repeat to members of my team. We create goals and agendas with everything we do. Seriously, this is so important! Meetings without clear-cut goals and agendas soon dissolve into chaos.

When you write something down on paper, you have added incentive to keep your commitment. Put this process in place before you launch a company. Build this into the cultural DNA of your team, and this will eliminate any confusion you might have.

I encourage my team to track every area of their lives. At the start of each year, I hand out a sheet of paper to each member on our team. Together, we write down the goals we have and stick this paper somewhere we'll remember to see it. For me, it's my wallet. "Be nicer to your wife." "Do more push-ups." "Lose weight." "Sell $50 million." All these are resolutions I carry with me everywhere I go.

To be successful, you must have goals.

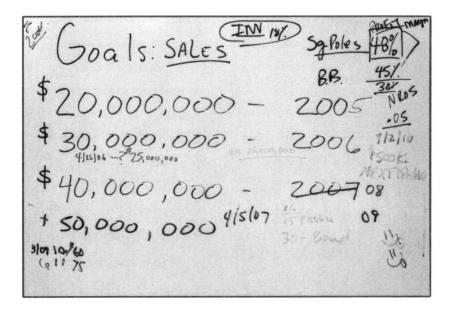

TIP 2: GO AFTER WHAT YOU DESIRE

There are all kinds of goals I make for my team. I write plans and share them with those in my company. I share them with people in my circle. This helps people think, see the big picture, and know where we are going. Together we plan, strategize, and ask what it will take to move the ball forward.

Here is a brief example that I will detail later. For years I had my eye on a form of nonwelded connection called Permalok. A company near us had a patent on it, but several years ago, the patent expired. Because I saw there was so much untapped potential, I focused a great deal of time and energy to make this product a success. In the end, we are going to make a ton (yes, that's a steel pun) of money on this innovation. However, there have been several bumps along the way.

But each day I keep showing up. I know what I want and will not stop until I have fulfilled my goals and dreams. And then, when I have, I'll add new ones! The chase never stops.

TIP 3: LEARN EARLY AND LEARN FAST

Some people are so afraid of failure they never take any action. They are in constant ready, aim mode and never fire. Just the other day, I talked to a guy who shared with me a few books he was reading. One of them said failure was bad and that it was critical entrepreneurs experience early success. While I agree success is good, I couldn't have disagreed more with this author's take on failure.

> Some people are so afraid of failure they never take any action.

It has been out of failure and some of the lowest moments of my life that I have experienced the most growth. My mom's death when I was fourteen years of age was hard. Still, I grew as a result. Terrible days in business cause me to go home and pull the covers over my eyes. But the next day I wake up and tell myself that today is going to be a great day. I move forward. Failure is often what drives me to tackle the next challenge.

No entrepreneur opens their doors and is perfect at operation and scaling a business. You learn through action and repetition.

I have lost count of the number of mistakes I have made at Trinity. But it is these same mistakes that pushed me toward success. Without them, I would have never learned. The key is to learn from your mistakes before your company scales to a size where mistakes are costly.

TIP 4: SURROUND YOURSELF WITH A STRONG TEAM

Several minds are better than one. You need to have a mastermind group and people you trust. Through having people in your corner, you can be much stronger than going it alone. Ask questions. Don't fall in love with yourself when things go well.

An outstanding example of this is my assistant, Phyllis. She has been the one constant at Trinity. She was our first employee and has served alongside me for forty-two years. To this day, I lean on her for advice. If I have questions about an employee, I run them by her. As I often say, when you find a keeper, treat them right and serve them well. Then you will have a lifelong friend.

When I first started hiring people to the Trinity team, I flew by the seat of my pants. I guessed at which employees would do well and which ones would not. Often, I was wrong. Today we use personality assessments and look at a broader pool of candidates. Instead of looking at just a few people, we interview twenty and run them through a CAD (challenge, assessment, and development) profile. While this slows down our hiring process and makes things a bit more complicated, in the end, this has proved effective.

We put a process in place and have built upon it. The result is that our employee satisfaction has increased while our turnover rate has declined.

TIP 5: REMEMBER THAT IT IS YOU AGAINST THE WORLD

The moment I stepped away from my previous company and started Trinity was the moment I realized I was all alone.

No other company had our best interest in mind. They were competing for their share of the market and had their own problems to worry about. In the years following Sal's departure from our company, I watched as massive companies like Valley Steel went under, all because they could not adapt. This continues to happen today with industries, such as when oil and gas pipelines are replaced with cleaner sources of energy.

Every time another company goes out of business, it reminds me of my own organization's fragility. If giants in our industry could go under after being in business for seventy years, who was I to think this would never happen to me?

While you never want to live in a place of constant suspicion, it is critical that every entrepreneur take ownership of their business. One way I have done this at Trinity is through not being reliant on other companies for survival. We manufacture our own pipe and sell our products directly to consumers. This places us in the driver's seat, and that is exactly where we want to be.

TIP 6: YOU DO NOT HAVE A SUSTAINABLE BUSINESS UNLESS IT CAN SCALE

After Trinity surpassed the $10 million mark in annual sales, I felt pretty good about myself and the direction we were headed. It was about that time my banker friend, Chuck, gave me a dose of reality.

He took one look at the structure of our company and said, "Robert, you don't have a business. You *are* the business." He was right. If something happened to me that day and I could not lead, the company might fold. This was something I could not deny, and it was also something I resolved to change.

My friend Jack Stack points out that $20 million companies are often the ones that get bought out. It's at that point we cannot conduct business as usual. You must build systems so that one person is not the sole key to the organization's success.

TIP 7: TREAT PEOPLE THE RIGHT WAY

I am a simple person and one who believes solid principles never go out of style. Make good decisions, be honest with others, and treat people the right way. Whenever I work with a client and sense I might not deliver a shipment on time, I let them know right away.

Because of my previous experiences, I make it a point to never put my hand in an employee's financial pocket. If anyone feels I have slighted them, I go out of my way to overcompensate them. Sometimes this has been costly, but I always want to take the high ground.

I am in life for the long haul.

Conclusion

I started this chapter with a story about getting cheated out of my $5,000 commission check and how that moment spurred me on to start Trinity Products.

When I set out on my own, my former boss, Bill, reached out and informed me I would never make it in the steel industry. The competition was too tough, I lacked experience, and it was only a matter of time before we shut our doors.

Fast-forward several years and Trinity was doing well. One afternoon I received a call, and my secretary said, "Robert, Bill is on the phone." Out of respect, I picked up the phone and answered.

"Robert—Bill here. Listen, I'm looking for a job. Would you be interested in hiring?"

I wasn't at that time, and we ended the conversation on a courteous note.

As I did, I couldn't help but think to myself about the full-circle nature of life. Only a few years before, this man had cheated me out of $5,000 and told me I would never make it. Now I could offer him a job. The sense of irony was profound.

Looking back, not only am I glad I took the high road in this relationship, but I'm glad I took the leap into something new. What looked like a bad situation at the time turned out to be a tremendous blessing in disguise.

Takeaways

➡ As a leader, think about times where you were fair or took the high road.

➡ Can you—or have you—dedicated yourself to the highest work ethic possible? If not, write out a plan on how you could improve in that area.

➡ Can you give examples of business or career opportunities that you've seen but haven't acted upon?

➡ Are there modifications to your company or business that you can identify? If so, write out a plan, save it, and share it with the leadership team or group when the time is right.

➡ Remember, you are always selling. If you're not selling yourself, who will? Your boss will if you make him your customer and his life easier.

➡ What are some of the failures you've experienced, and what did you learn from them?

➡ Can you list some ways to take yourself out of making every decision? This is the only way the business will grow, and you'll grow into a leader instead of a doer.

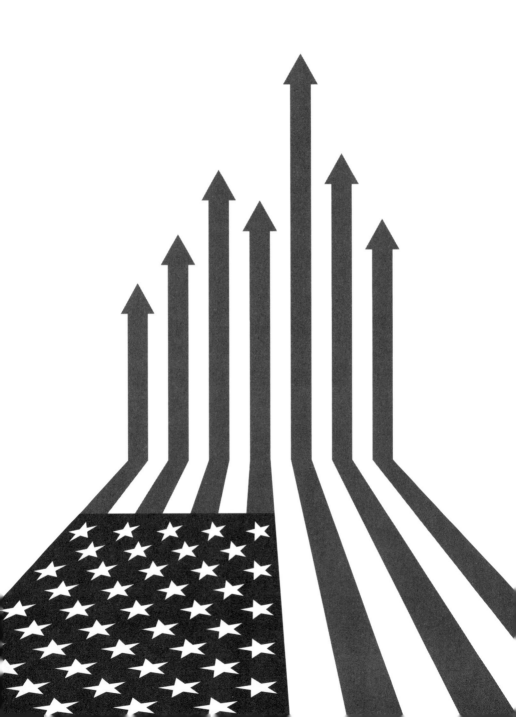

CHAPTER 2

BUILD A SALES TEAM YOU CAN TRUST

Around twenty years ago, I was driving my fifth-grade son home from school. As we moved along in our SUV, I was on the phone with a client. We were negotiating back and forth on some numbers, and after I hung up, AJ leaned forward and asked me a thought-provoking question.

"Dad, did you just lie to that guy?"

I was dumbfounded and asked him what he meant.

"Well, my friends at school say all salespeople lie to earn a living. It's just what they do."

AJ wasn't trying to be mean or put down my profession. He was simply stating what he thought was an obvious fact. All salespeople lie, and the ones who say they don't are double liars.

It was a statement I had heard before, but listening to my son repeat it that day did something for me. It touched a nerve, and that moment turned into a teaching lesson. I explained to my son that while some salespeople did lie, the best ones were committed to truth. And over the years since that car ride home, we have had many conversations on this subject. We have talked about countless principles that drive the way I do business, live my life as a salesperson, and work to become a better human being. And it's these very ideas I want to share with you in this chapter.

Sales is everything. I often say you can tell the strength of an organization by its ability to accurately project sales and expenses. If you have no sales, you have no company. It is the oxygen that allows organizations to breathe.

My journey into the sales world started in 1973.

Catching the Sales Bug

Between my senior year of high school and freshman year of college at Mizzou, I took a summer job with Southwestern Publishing Company out of Nashville, going door to door selling Bibles, Bible encyclopedias, and dictionaries. Together with my friends Tommy and Mark, we set out to have a fun adventure and hopefully make a lot of money. Instead it turned into a tough life lesson.

Southwestern Publishing Company was a great business that took young college kids in, taught them to sell in a one-week training course, and then sent them on their way. They loved these words from Calvin Coolidge:

> *"Nothing in this world can take the place of persistence. Talent will not; nothing is more common than unsuccessful men with talent. Genius will not; unrewarded genius is almost a proverb. Education will not; the world is full of educated derelicts. Persistence and determination alone are*

omnipotent. The slogan Press On! has solved and always will solve the problems of the human race."

This philosophy wormed its way into everything we did. I discovered that attitude, persistence, and determination always win the day. Being young and inexperienced, I thought sales would be a piece of cake. *How hard could it be to sell Bibles in the Bible Belt?* I thought to myself. Little did I know.

After my training in Nashville was complete, my two friends and I moved into a minister's basement in Erlanger, Kentucky (just outside Cincinnati), for ten dollars per week. A different time.

Our initial plan was to work for twelve weeks with no days off. On Sundays, we met up with other salespeople from other regions to compare notes and see how we could improve. This taught me the value of continuous improvement. Because I loved working hard and was used to long hours, the opportunity to have unlimited income potential was appealing. This was better than life on the farm, where I made only two dollars an hour. Now the lid was off the ceiling, and the more I sold, the more I earned.

Aside from food, we never spent any money. We were too tired to do anything after we finished the day! Tommy was the only one out of the three of us who owned a car. And so he would drop me off at a location, and because we lived in a pre–cell phone era, we would plan a point and time to meet. There we would discuss how our days went and have dinner.

Our trio turned into a duo after a week, when Mark opted out. He discovered what Tommy and I were realizing—not everyone in the greater Cincinnati area was excited to see a Bible salesperson at their door. This proved disheartening at times. We had people who were nasty to us and propositioned us, and we even had a few homeowners pull out guns.

Still, these experiences taught us invaluable life lessons on the importance of persistence. We discovered what it meant to parachute into a community and survive. Our encounters with mean homeowners taught us people skills and the importance of "killing people with kindness." As the weeks passed, our confidence continued to grow, and our sales got better and better.

Here are a few of the lessons we learned:

- **Lesson 1:** If someone did not respond to our three-step sales pitch, we moved on. We realized it was a numbers game. Some would buy; others would not. There was no point wasting time and energy on someone who was unlikely to make a purchase. Not everyone could be sold a product, and some people disliked salespeople altogether. In situations like this, there was nothing we could do but be nice and move on.

- **Lesson 2:** Never skip a house. Ever. We used to say it was the house we skipped that was the house we sold. This one time there was a house down a long gravel road. Nothing inside me wanted to walk the half-mile hike just to hear one more no. So I passed it by and continued to the next door. But the farther I stepped away, the louder that voice inside my head told me I had made the wrong decision. After a few more steps, I turned back, and to my surprise I sold an entire set of Bible encyclopedias—the big money sell. Again, this taught me an important lesson. Do not skip a step in the process. There are no shortcuts to success.

- **Lesson 3:** You can motivate yourself and keep yourself up with positive affirmations. Door-to-door sales is tough. Every morning, while I was in the shower, I would say to myself, "This is going to be a great day" (a practice I used this morning). Between houses, I would mumble to myself, "I can, I will, and I'm going to!" At first these motivational sentences seemed silly, but these techniques helped me get through some hard and lonely moments. They helped me move forward on those days I wanted to quit.

- **Lesson 4:** I am in charge of my happiness. Door-to-door sales taught me people are attracted to happiness and positivity. This is something only I can control. If I show up to work with a negative attitude, this pollutes everything I do. But if I arrive with a positive mindset, others will follow my lead.

My summer with Southwestern Publishing ended, and in my mind, I received a master's degree in sales, people, and hard knocks. As a kid from a small town with very little experience, I was the most confident I'd ever been. There was nothing I could not do or accomplish. The world was mine, and it was one of the most powerful feelings I had ever felt!

In the end, my earnings were less than if I had remained on the farm. I earned $1,200 but had to deduct $200 of this due to bad checks (an irony given the product I was selling). This left me with $1,000—about $400 less than I would have made on the farm.

My first venture as a salesperson was a huge learning experience. And even though I saw limited success, I knew I was going to be involved in some type of sales for the rest of my life. I was hooked.

Be Relational Instead of Transactional

My time selling Bibles taught me the art of being a great salesperson always starts with the ability to build relationships. If I could not build strong rapport with my customers, there was no way I would ever make the sale.

Motivational speaker Patricia Fripp writes, "You don't close a sale; you open a relationship." This is a point I drive home with my team every day. We live in a world that is much more instant than when I started Trinity. Back then I thought fax machines were great. Now there is instant streaming, instant online ordering, and instant availability.

With this heightened spontaneity, businesses have become more transactional and less relational. They have taken note of companies like Amazon and make everything about a process. It's all about getting people to click on a service, sign up for a subscription, and complete the transaction.

On small items, this might be just what the customer needs. For example, if I'm purchasing dog food or toilet paper online, I have little desire to have a relationship with the distributer.

But for any purchase of consequence—such as a home renovation or vehicle repair—I want to know the people involved. It's not about finding the person with the lowest transactional cost. Instead it's about finding someone who will get the job done and work with me if there is an issue. It's finding someone I trust.

Because much of the business world has opted for transactional interactions, I see this as a great opportunity. As Jill Rowley notes, "Before LinkedIn and other social networks, in the sales world, ABC stood for Always Be Closing. Now it means Always Be Connecting."[1] Big difference! I love closing, but I also believe in the power of connecting.

---

1   Jill Rowley, "The ABCs of Social Selling: Always Be Connected," last modified February 27, 2013, https://blogs.oracle.com/marketingcloud/post/the-abcs-of-social-selling-always-be-connected.

Customers are looking for relationships. They want people who care. Building great relationships takes time and involves some pain. It's certainly not an overnight strategy for success. It's a long-term approach. But over time the benefits of great relationships compound and far outweigh the pain.

Every business goes through its share of tough times. But when those seasons hit, it's the companies that have created strong relationships with their employees and customers that make it through. When you build a foundation for your company based on trust, you can stand against anything that comes your way.

> **When you build a foundation for your company based on trust, you can stand against anything that comes your way.**

Tell the Truth

Jack Stack says, "You simply can't operate unless people believe you and believe one another."[2] Trust is established as people in your company tell the truth. When my son asked me if salespeople lied, that conversation prompted action. I began to ask myself this: "What if everyone on our team had a high commitment to honesty? What if words like *truth* and *integrity* were qualities we took seriously?"

At this point in my career, I was committed to truth. But I didn't see any way I could enforce this with members on my team. It was one of those ideas that seemed great in concept but a nightmare to apply. Deep down, I knew members on my team did lie and fudge the truth.

---

2   Jack Stack and Bo Burlingham, *The Great Game of Business, Expanded and Updated: The Only Sensible Way to Run a Company* (New York: Crown Publishing, 2013), 56.

But about five years after my conversation with my son AJ, I took the plunge and laid down the now-famous rule in our company, "If you lie, you're fired." As I outlined to my team, "I can fix a mistake, but I cannot fix a lie."

By this point I was fed up with what little white lies did to our culture. A little holding back of the truth here and there created too many nightmare scenarios and resulted in more damage than the original mistake someone covered up! While many organizations tolerate lies of this nature, I knew this was not something I could accept if we were going to ascend to where I thought we needed to go.

Initially, this new rule came with pushback. My closest team members said, "Robert, if we do this, everyone on our team is going to be fired or quit." I could see their point. Sometimes salespeople get put on the spot and say anything that comes to mind just to get off the phone. They might respond with, "Yes, it shipped," or "Yes, we're going to make that delivery on time," when the truth is something different. They want to please the customer but wind up creating a major problem in the process.

Rather than pulling back on my new rule, I instituted an exemption clause called "You can recant before your boss finds out." Sometimes members of our team were placed in tough jams where they felt compelled to lie or fudge the truth. They might be put on the spot, and their fear of saying the wrong thing compelled them to lie. In these situations, I gave them the chance to recant. If a member of my team lied, but they came forward and admitted their lie before they were caught, I extended them grace.

If they made an overcommitment to a customer, I would have them call back and tell the truth. "John, I messed up. I told you we could make that delivery next week, but I can't make the commitment." Then I coached them so they knew what to do the next time they were put on the spot.

Instead of saying what the customer wanted to hear in the moment, I taught them to admit what they didn't know. "Hey, I'm not sure about this. Let me follow up with my boss, and I'll get back to you in a few minutes." This offered a few minutes to regroup and bring their boss into the picture. It's the perfect out and prevented a boatload of lies.

Salespeople must have courage and confidence in the whole team to be this kind of person. Most organizations are not transparent and do not value their customers enough to tell them the truth. As a leader, you must build a solid culture so that everyone steps up and tells the truth.

No one gets fired at our company for messing up. Mistakes are easy to correct. Lies are unacceptable. Again, while policies like this might not be popular and cause your employees to feel a bit uncomfortable, in the end, you create a culture of trust. At Trinity, our team feels safe. They know that if they mess up, their boss has their back. They're not going to get thrown under the bus for a problem that can be fixed.

This brings to mind a painful example.

Five Thousand Calls to Alaska

The critical call number for our salespeople has always been fifty calls a day. That was what we thought it took to move the needle. Fifty calls meant approximately three inquiries, which generally led to one sale. This formula worked for me, and I knew it was something attainable.

When we stumbled across this magic number, we began tracking each salesperson's progress, posting the number of sales calls per day. This created a strong culture of accountability.

Unfortunately, one of our savvy vets, whom we'll call Jim, found a way to game the system. For years Jim always led the team in calls. And in many of our team meetings, I held Jim up as an example to the group.

Jim's sales numbers were great. He wasn't at the top of the chart, but he was close. To me, he was everything we were about. Hardworking, diligent, and consistent over time. But as it turned out, Jim wasn't telling the entire story.

In 2010, we decided to change phone companies. We found out our current provider had been overcharging us for some time, and we conducted an internal audit. In those days, before unlimited calling, our monthly bills were through the roof. One Friday afternoon, when I was talking to the employee who conducted the audit, she said something that threw me for a loop.

"Robert, did you know someone in the office made five thousand calls to Time and Temperature in Anchorage, Alaska, last year?" I couldn't believe my ears. Five thousand calls? Why would someone do that?

"Who was it?" I asked, more than a little puzzled.

"It's Jim, the sales guy," was the response.

A knot formed in my stomach, and all I could think was that my employee on the other end of the line was mistaken. I knew Jim. He was a good guy and the perfect poster child for our organization. If word got out that his numbers were all a facade, what would members of my team think? Would I lose credibility? Would my message be devalued?

There was no doubt this revelation presented a dilemma and tested my commitment to truth. Jim was one of our best salespeople. Yes, he was a liar. But he got the job done. Didn't the ends justify the means? But even as I wrestled with these questions in my mind, I knew what the answer had to be.

Monday morning, I fired him. In doing so, we lost a productive team member but took one step closer toward a stronger culture.

Because there aren't many secrets in our industry, word soon got around about what had happened, and I took my share of friendly gibes. Six months later, I was in Chicago at the Drake Hotel at the National Association of Steel Pipe Distributors convention. After one of our sessions, I walked into a local bar and came across some of my pipe buddies. After a few drinks, they started telling me a story that sounded all too familiar—a story that involved some guy who made five thousand calls to Time and Temperature in Alaska.

Rather than trying to cover it up and act surprised, I just laughed and told them the truth. In doing so, I became the brunt of a few jokes, but that was just fine with me. Telling the truth is more important than my ego. In the words of Brian Tracy, it's called eating the frog.

If I were told to eat a frog (something I hope to avoid for the remainder of my life), I'd do my best to finish the job as soon as possible. I'd take one big gulp and swallow it whole. No nibbling or second thinking. It's the same with life. Sometimes telling the truth or owning up to a problem is painful. But in those moments, eat the frog and eat it quickly.

Every morning, there are figurative frogs that await every member of our team. They are those things everyone dreads. Rather than sitting on them till midafternoon, I tell our team to get them out of the way at the start of their day. Face that awkward conversation, call that angry client, fix that problem. If you don't, the issue will continue to weigh on your mind and make you less productive.

When you get these frogs off your desk, you free up your mind to focus on the most important issues instead of fearing what's about to happen. This is a principle I apply to all of life. Whenever I have a problem at home or with a colleague, I face it as soon as possible. Over the years, this has led to a lifetime of great relationships.

The quicker you adopt this principle, the easier your life will get!

Hire the Right People

While sales come naturally to me, this is not the same story with others. It did not take many sales hires at Trinity for me to realize I was not a great predictor of sales success.

I didn't understand it. I would hire fifty people, and only five of them would last. It was tough to help others see what was second nature to me. All the intangibles of making a sale, which I thought all salespeople possessed, were often missing in the candidates we hired.

In 2015 this changed. My son Bo became assistant sales manager and began incorporating personality profiles into our testing. This made a huge difference.

We use what is called a cultural index, and we build ideal profiles of every sales position on our team. Then we interview potential candidates based on this profile. These initial interviews are conducted over the phone, followed by an online test.

If we don't receive the scores we like, we move on to another candidate. By that point, we estimate the odds of them being a fit for our company are low and hiring them would likely result in a waste of time.

Hiring is hard work. There was so much I had to learn. Unfortunately, many companies settle for less because the hirer doesn't want to devote the time necessary to land a quality individual. There is too much work to be done and not enough time to think about who will be a good fit. But this type of thinking is terribly shortsighted.

It's taken a few years, but I now realize it's worth it to invest the time and energy on the front end to create a more sustainable result.

If your organization struggles with a high turnover rate on its sales team, my challenge to you is to take a step back and make sure you aren't cheating the process. If you are, you will set yourself up to have a lot of do-overs. It's a lesson most companies never learn.

While the personality profiling did not guarantee a perfect hire, it increased our odds. We went from batting .100 to hitting .500. Of the people we selected, 50 percent of them exceeded $100,000 a year in sales. The others struggled and often did not last more than a few years.

I'm often asked, "What makes a great salesperson?" The answer isn't obvious, and the process of selection is rather nonscientific. One of the reasons it's tough to hire great salespeople is that there are so many intangibles. Are they great at building relationships? Do they have *presence* when they walk into a room? Will they be persistent when times are tough? Is their primary goal to clock in and earn a paycheck or work beyond quitting time and build a career? Are they teachable? These are questions only time and evaluation can answer.

Passion is a big one for me. I've learned I can guide people who are misguided, but I cannot drag people to where they need to go. I'm not going to waste my time and energy pushing someone along. This is one of the reasons I love to hire young people who were the captains of their sports teams. They might not have made it to the big time, but they have developed the key components of a winning culture—hard drive, work ethic, team skills, and a desire to win!

In *Talking to Strangers*, Malcolm Gladwell notes, "We think we can easily see into the hearts of others based on the flimsiest of clues."[3] This is true. In the early days, I thought I could tell which salespeople would make it and which ones would not. Now I just accept that there is no way to bat 1.000. I'm going to make a lot of misses, and the best I can do is try to limit these misses as much as possible.

> I've stopped looking for people who sound smart, dress well, and look like they can do the job. Now I seek out people who have an entrepreneurial spirit and have the passion to lead and innovate. If they have these pieces in place, everything else can be taught.

I've stopped looking for people who sound smart, dress well, and look like they can do the job. Now I seek out people who have an entrepreneurial spirit and have the passion to lead and innovate. If they have these pieces in place, everything else can be taught.

Takeaways

➡ Remember, you're always selling (or you should be)!

➡ List ways you're persistent toward your goals.

➡ Remember any times that you skipped a step in the process or took a shortcut and it backfired. Write them out and explain what you learned from it.

---

3   Malcolm Gladwell, *Talking to Strangers: What We Should Know about the People We Don't Know* (Boston: Little, Brown and Publishing Company, 2019).

➡ You're in charge of your own happiness. What can you do to make yourself happier? Make a list and think hard about it.

➡ Make a list of people, companies, or customers you should be building relationships with—and get started right now!

➡ Think of times you've told your boss or a customer something that wasn't quite true and it hurt your relationship. What could you have done differently? Pledge to pause before you say something, and instead say, "Let me get back to you."

➡ How much energy do you spend on hiring the right person? If not enough, why?

➡ If you're having to constantly drag someone up, you *have to* move on without them.

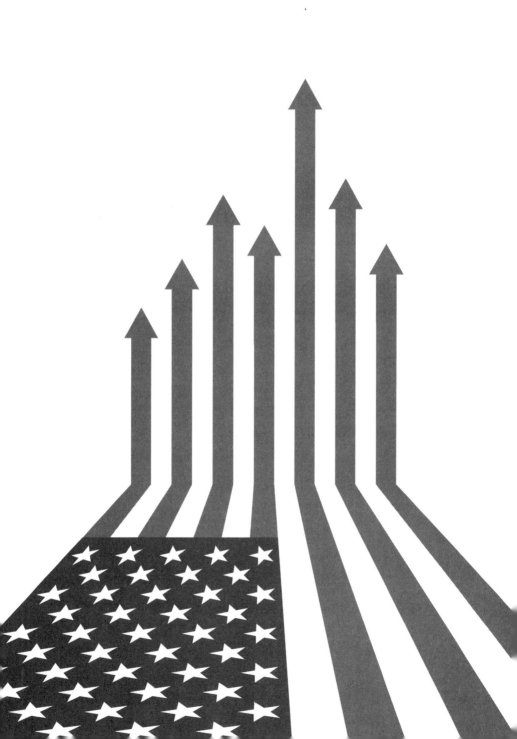

CHAPTER 3

FLIP THE PYRAMID

Foundation is everything. If your foundation is strong, your organization is built to last. If your foundation is weak, it will be only a matter of time before your structure crumbles. All the heavy lifting in an organization is done at a foundational level.

Since our company's origin, Trinity has supplied steel to some of the most important foundations in America. We had the privilege of supplying steel for the slurry wall surrounding the new World Trade Center, and over the past forty years we have provided structural components for the Javits Center in Manhattan, LaGuardia Airport in Queens, Paulsboro Marine Terminal in New Jersey, the Bay Bridge in San Francisco, and almost every major bridge in the United States!

In a literal way, Trinity Products has been foundational in holding this great country together, and it is the reason we became the number one supplier of large-diameter twenty-four-inch-and-above structural pipe in America.

Because most of my time is spent dealing with components that hold a structure together, I know that foundation is everything—in buildings and in business—and this brings to mind an illustration not far from where I live.

The Eads Bridge

Trinity Products is located in O'Fallon, Missouri, approximately forty-five minutes from St. Louis. While most people who think of St. Louis today picture the Gateway Arch, there is another piece of construction that served as the true gateway for westward expansion.

Being in the steel business myself, I am a student of this industry. So bear with me for a brief history lesson! Following the Civil War, the expansion of railroads across the United States exploded. Within a few short years, the US went from having a shortage of viable travel routes to having more tracks than supply and demand could support. Between 1863 and 1869 the first transcontinental railroad was completed, linking California to New York. It was a tremendous breakthrough and did much to hold our great nation together. That said, there was a challenge that arose.

The "Gateway to the West" was impeded by the vast width of the Mississippi River. This presented itself as a major obstacle for early pioneers making the journey across the land. Then came along two individuals, James Eads and Andrew Carnegie. One possessed the engineering expertise, and the other was blessed with a tremendous amount of financial capital. Eads had been a local resident of St. Louis for some time and was familiar with the geographical landscape. He knew that for a bridge to have success, the foundation needed to be strong.

Up until that point, bridges were made of wood or iron. But with the powerful current of the Mississippi River, constructing a bridge out of either of these two elements would result in disaster. Wood would eventually warp or rot, and iron would prove to be too brittle over such an extended range.

That is when Eads had an idea. Why not construct the bridge out of steel? As someone who had worked in the salvage industry, digging boats from the depths of the Mississippi, Eads was unique in that he was familiar with the riverbed in a way that few men of his day were. He knew that the only way the bridge would last was if it were securely anchored to bedrock. In some areas, this was not as problematic. In other areas, this meant digging down through over a hundred feet of sand.

But Eads and his workers kept at it. He constructed pneumatic caissons, which were essentially a massive steel tube that allowed workers to be able to descend a spiral staircase to the floor of the riverbed and anchor the bridge to bedrock. He implemented the use of chromium-molybdenum steel for the first time, and this gave the bridge added strength. And he constructed tubular arch systems for the archways that ensured the bridge would not warp over time.[4]

Eads's goal was to construct a bridge that lasted for as long as people found it useful to remain in existence.[5] To this end his project was a remarkable success, and the bridge was completed in 1874. Today people continue to find his bridge useful, and the old saying remains true: a solid foundation is the gift that keeps on giving!

---

4   David Lobbig, "The Eads Bridge," Missouri Historical Society. Accessed June 1, 2021, https://www.youtube.com/watch?v=Pwrhept8G_Q&ab_channel=MissouriHistoricalSociety.

5   Ibid.

Your Employees Are Your Foundation

Employees are the foundation of every organization, and I have come to realize that the success of every organization rises and falls based on the heavy lifting done by the team "below the surface."

Because this is the case, it is why I am serious about investing in my team's well-being and doing whatever I can to give them the support needed. Just as it would be foolish to build a bridge without taking into careful account the foundation, so it is foolish to build an organization without considering the most important component that makes it function.

> Employees are the foundation of every organization, and I have come to realize that the success of every organization rises and falls based on the heavy lifting done by the team "below the surface."

Unfortunately, we grow accustomed to looking at all the wrong locations and missing what takes place behind the scenes. I suppose it is human nature to eat an apple from a tree and fail to appreciate the roots that have given this fruit life. This is why we as leaders must shift our mindset. In the words of John Maxwell, "Leadership is influence." And as leaders, we influence our teams in either positive or negative ways.

Only when leaders commit to positive influence can they lay a strong foundation and create an organization that sets their employees up for success.

Start with Those Who Are Engaged

Admittedly, this is not always easy, but a great place to start is by asking questions. Every two weeks I sit down with the heads of my various departments at Trinity and ask them how they are doing their jobs and to list three ways we as a team can do better. This is a culture meeting where I am instilling organizational DNA into the lives of those on my team.

No topic of improvement is struck off the list until everyone agrees on a solution. From there we organize the right machinery, monetize accordingly, and prioritize how we will make their suggestions a reality. This gives people on our team meaningful input. They know I take their suggestions seriously because I take *them* seriously.

From my vantage point, it is my goal as the founder and president of the organization to remove obstacles that prevent members of my team from having the success they can achieve.

To do this, I work hard at speaking the language of each of my departments. I want to know what the culture is like in all areas of my business. Most leaders and companies do not take the time to do this, and the result is an organization where the culture is unhealthy, with many on the team feeling disgruntled and confused.

If this is the situation you find yourself in today, there is hope. My suggestion to you would be to start with those members on your team who *are* engaged. Seek out those people who clock out at four but stick around till four thirty. Find those diamonds in the rough who go above and beyond to do their jobs with excellence every day.

You need people on your team who care!

Unfortunately, most job recruiters get sucked into the eye test when they hire. They see the person who is good looking, in shape, and well dressed, and they assume they will grow into their role to be the best person for their job. It's why attractive men and women make on average 12 percent more than those who are not.[6] When we look at someone, we cannot help but allow our judgment to cloud what we see and hear.

But at Trinity we hire and retain based on performance and engagement. If an employee is engaged, it is much more likely they will stick around for the long haul. Because we believe this so strongly, my team does their absolute best to guard against hiring out of any sense of bias.

For example, my sales team now conducts initial interviews with potential sales agents over the phone rather than in person or through video calls. The reason for this is simple. It will be their job to sell themselves to customers over the phone, and if they cannot do it with us, they are in trouble. Over the phone their slick physique or well-tailored suit will do them little good. They must be able to perform under pressure and be engaged in the process.

To this point, several years ago I had an individual at Trinity who was a welder, which for us is a very important position. Talented as he was, Ronny didn't necessarily pass what you might call the "eye test." His long hair and tattoos meant that he was not going to serve as the model for our company website anytime soon. That said, I remember having a roundtable discussion that told me all I needed to know about his level of engagement.

At a point in our history when we faced the threat of a looming recession, Ronny looked up at me and stated, "Hey, wait a second. If the interest rates are going down, doesn't this mean our interest expense is going to be lower?"

---

6   Drake Baer, "This Cognitive Bias Explains Why Pretty People Make 12% More Money Than Everybody Else," accessed June 1, 2021, https://www.businessinsider.com/halo-effect-money-beauty-bias-2014-11.

I immediately latched on to his answer because it was so profound, demonstrated his recognition, and showed me he cared. He got it and wanted to make sure he did all he could to ensure our entire team improved.

When you start hiring for engagement, your team will soon comprise people who care. And the way you help your employees care is by including them. Talk to the people actually doing the jobs and ask for their advice. Ask for input on new products and design. This gives them a better sense of purpose and also allows you to gain better insight on future products and goals.

Create a Culture of Mutual Accountability

As you start engaging members of your team in the process and empowering them to live out their unique skills and attributes in your organization, your life will become easier.

This is the hidden secret many leaders fail to recognize. They feel life at the top can be managed only with a tight fist—that to give too much leeway to those on their team will create a culture of chaos when just the opposite is true. They have bought in to the old saying that if you want something done right you must do it yourself!

Do not misunderstand my point. By empowering those on our team, I am not calling leaders to stand down and cheer from the sidelines. No, it is critical that company strategy comes from the top. But I believe input from the troops gives this strategy power, and the key is that this strategy trickles down to every department in the organization.

It is the leader's responsibility to gather all the facts and data, discuss this with members of their team, and then formulate a plan that gets passed down to every member on the team. This should be a universal plan that everyone can support. For a strategy to be successful, it must feel as though this decision was made by everyone on the team.

When the entire team makes a decision, a culture of mutual accountability takes place. At Trinity Products, we hold everyone on the team accountable regardless of their position. Accountability is a major ingredient in teamwork and success.

This is important, because it has been my experience that employees tend to think they are doing more than others when this is seldom the case. Instead, they often have a warped perspective of their role and the roles they perceive others on the team play. But when folks have to sit in when someone else is out, they soon discover everyone's job is difficult in its own way.

When everyone is on the same page, we all pull our weight together. And with this system in place, we lay out ways to hold individuals and departments accountable to everyone in the organization. There will be no more "we do this" and "they did that." We are a team pulling in the same direction and sharing in the fruits of our labors.

Teams that work together can accomplish so much more because they operate based on fact, not speculation. When those on the team do not receive the resources they were promised, they can voice their concerns to those in leadership, and change can occur. They hold leadership accountable.

By creating a culture of accountability in both directions, you craft an organization that makes everyone's lives better. This accountability becomes the currency of your leadership and business.

Mottoes That Guide My Interactions

A common theme of my life is consistency over time. As Darren Hardy writes in his book *The Compound Effect*, "You will never change your life until you change something you do daily. The secret of your success is found in your daily routine."[7] This is why I say business is easy, but it's the daily execution that's so hard.

It's not about redesigning the wheel and coming up with an entirely new method that has never been tried before. Rather it's about doing the little things well every single day—over and over and over again! There's joy in staying the course and having the toughness to turn routine into success.

In my life I have compiled a list of mottoes or core values that shape my interactions with others. They hold my feet to the fire and remind me to put my team first. The first of these is one I have alluded to already in this chapter.

MOTTO 1: THE MORE YOU GIVE, THE MORE YOU RECEIVE

For our team, this is more than just a statement. It guides the way we behave and interact. We truly believe the more we give to others, the more we receive in the long run. Because this philosophy is so ingrained in our cultural DNA, we make a conscious decision to give above and beyond what is expected of us.

Personally, I made the decision years ago to never leave another person feeling as though they were shortchanged in our interaction. I chose this path because I have experienced the pain of being short-changed myself, and it does not feel great.

---

7   Darren Hardy, *The Compound Effect: Jumpstart Your Income, Your Life, Your Success* (Bhopal, India: Manjul Publishing, 2012).

At times this decision has cost me financially, but the peace of mind I have gained in the process has been well worth the investment. Even when feedback is negative and I feel my generosity has not been well received, I continue to make giving a lifestyle. I don't allow negative feedback in the past to shortchange others in the future.

I made the decision years ago to never leave another person feeling as though they were short-changed in our interaction.

Secretly, I give because I am selfish. I give because it makes me feel good in the process! When I help make the lives of those around me easier, *my* life gets better. So, in an odd way, I am selfish. I help others because I receive pleasure doing so in the process.

MOTTO 2: IF YOU CANNOT FIND TALENT, CULTIVATE IT

Cultivating talent is difficult and requires a large investment of time and energy. But sometimes options are limited. When this is the case, it is a good leader's responsibility to step up and take the team to the next level.

Unfortunately, many leaders keep bad employees around because the leaders are lazy and don't feel they have the time to find someone new. But it's best to conserve all the time and energy this employee will drag out of you and just move on. Have the difficult conversation and stop putting off the inevitable so that you can do something else that is more enjoyable in the moment.

Initially, I did not do this well, and it took me a while to adjust. But when I made the switch, it made a huge difference. I have since learned to knock out the difficult tasks fast and early. I eat the frog, always keeping in mind that the next person I hire might be the best employee of my life!

Whenever I can, I try to promote from within. In fact, almost all our leadership group has come from our regular shop floor hires. These folks we hired were already leaders at heart but just hadn't gotten much of an opportunity at their young ages to demonstrate what they could do.

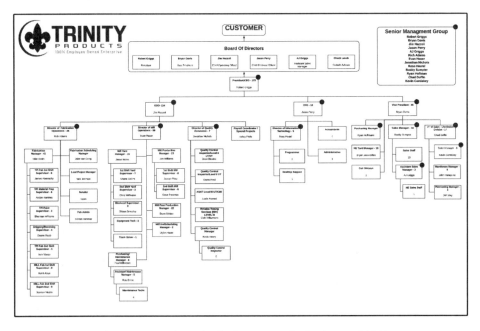

It's impressive what a leadership team we've built since 2000!

MOTTO 3: I'LL KNOW IT WHEN I SEE IT

There used to be a sign in my office that read, "I don't know what IT is but I'll know IT when I see it!"

Many times, as the interview process progresses, I have sat across the hiring table from someone who has applied to one of our positions and have internally shaken my head. "Nope, not this one," I've said to myself. "They just don't have the *it factor*."

After more than forty years in business, I have learned to trust my instincts. Sometimes people give off a vibe that tells me they are not on the same page. It might be something they say or do, and often I can't put my finger on it. Still, I just know we are not going to be a fit.

But when I find *it*, I reward it, grow it, and nurture it. Sometimes I make a mistake and misjudge people. This is all a part of the territory that comes with being a leader, and it is easy to become disheartened or disappointed when this happens. However, instead of beating myself up, I double down and keep moving forward, trusting that the next *it* will come along.

MOTTO 4: DO NOT ACCEPT DRAMA OR NEGATIVITY

Operating a business is hard, and you cannot be surrounded by people who are constantly bringing the team down.

If you are like I was, sometimes you get caught in the trap of saying, "What would I do without this person?" But this is actually a lazy approach. The real issue is that you are avoiding having a difficult conversation. Bottom line: if you think someone isn't the right fit, the situation is not going to change until you address it.

On more than one occasion, I will get out of a meeting with members of one of my departments and know something is wrong. I can tell something is not clicking. Someone on the team is not picking up the slack. Often, as we are leaving the room, one of my team members will come up to me and say something like, "RG, so-and-so doesn't have *it*!" With a nod, I acknowledge their statement and connect with the meaning behind it. In the words of the great Jim Collins, this so-and-so is not one of the right people on the bus, and either they need to be helped off or transitioned to a different seat.

Embracing the Heart of a Servant

The essence of being a great leader is taking on the heart of what Robert Greenleaf calls "servant leadership." It is placing others' best interests in front of our own.

This means serving everyone, starting with all the folks at the bottom of the org chart who help you get the product out the door every day. It's serving the customer, keeping in mind that they are your real boss. Everything you do as an organization should be with the intent of putting your employees and customers first. Without people, you cannot serve customers, and without customers, you do not have a business!

We will get into this more in the next chapter, but part of sharing involves sharing information and the profits of the business. This gets everyone engaged and keeps you focused on the team. By setting up the business to share in its success, you create the environment of ownership. This allows you as the leader to drive the business in whatever direction it needs to go, as you have a team of owners to share the load!

Now, I know you are going to say, "Why should I do that?" Here is the reason. By building a model of setting standards, both process-wise and financially, you can free yourself to grow the business and create more wealth and success for everyone. Again, the more you give, the more you receive. It works. Trust me!

All of this sets you up for great success and gives you the freedom to create, drive, and build something dynamic and of greater value to everyone. As you do this, post or scoreboard all the data you are measuring. Make it a point to show *everything* your team is doing. I say this because people always tend to think things are either worse or better than they are. In reality, results are generally right in the middle. They might not be great, but they are not terrible.

When information is shared freely across departmental lines, communication improves, and everyone feels as though they are on the same team.

Hint: because no one has taught them differently, employees tend to think businesses make a regular amount of profit every single month. They do not know any better, because no one has ever taught them different. Only as you show the choppiness of business will they start to learn and not worry when things are bad. This is something I have wrestled with over the years. As an owner, I do not want to unnecessarily worry or scare my employees and cause them to leave. And to be clear, some will! But the ones who are keepers will stick around because they see the big picture and see how they can share in the company's

> People always tend to think things are either worse or better than they are. In reality, results are generally right in the middle. They might not be great, but they are not terrible.

profits. Like you, they also read the paper, watch the news, and know when the economy is bad. This means that when you are honest and speak the truth, this only reinforces their faith in what you are doing!

Five Keys to Empowering Your Team

No leader has all the answers. But when you begin to collaborate and build a team, you start to get great answers, and everybody wins. When you invite everyone's input, you lay a strong foundation and build a relationship for success. But how do you do it? Here are five steps.

STEP 1: ACKNOWLEDGE EVERYONE'S JOB IS IMPORTANT

JOB DESCRIPTION

⊕Trinity Products, Inc.			Approved By:	**QAM**	
Document Title: **Job Description**			Page 1 of 2	Effective Date: 4/8/2015	
Document Type:	Document Number:	Initial Issue Date:	Revision:	Approve Date:	
Form	**F 5-4-1**	**4/8/2015**	**Original**	4/8/2015	

Job title	*Welder*
Reports to	

Duties and responsibilities

1) Welds together metal components of products, such as pipe, plate, rail, angle, rounds, as specified by layout, blueprints, diagram, work order, welding procedures, or oral instructions, using electric arc-welding equipment: Obtains specified electrode and inserts electrode into portable holder or threads consumable electrode wire through portable welding gun or automatic equipment

2) Connects cables from welding unit to obtain amperage, voltage, slope, and pulse, as specified by WELDING ENGINEER or WELDING TECHNICIAN.

3) Starts power supply to produce electric current.

4) Strikes arc which generates heat to melt and deposit metal from electrode to work piece and join edges of work piece.

5) Manually guides electrode or gun along weld line, maintaining length of arc and speed of movement to form specified depth of fusion and bead, as judged from color of metal, sound of weld, and size of molten puddle.

6) Welds in flat, horizontal, vertical, or overhead positions.

7) Examines weld for bead size and other specifications.

8) May manually apply filler rod to supply weld metal.

9) May clean or degrease weld joint or work piece, using wire brush, portable grinder, or chemical bath.

10) May repair broken or cracked parts and fill holes.

11) May prepare broken parts for welding by grooving or scarfing surfaces.

12) May chip off excess weld, slag, and spatter, using hand scraper or power chipper.

13) May preheat work piece, using hand torch or heating furnace.

14) May position and clamp work pieces together or assemble them in jig or fixture.

15) May tack assemblies together.

16) May cut metal plates or structural shapes.

17) May be designated according to type of equipment used as Welder, Carbon Arc; Welder, Flux-Cored Arc; Welder, Gas-Metal Arc; Welder, Gas-Tungsten Arc; Welder, Hand, Submerged Arc; Welder, Plasma Arc; Welder, Shielded-Metal Arc.

18) May operate other machine shop equipment to prepare components for welding.

19) May be designated according to product welded as Welder, Boilermaker.

20) Important variations include types of metals welded, sub processes used, trade name of equipment used, work site, method of application, high-production or custom, level of ambidexterity required, type of joints welded.

21) May be required to pass employer performance tests or standard tests to meet certification standards of governmental agencies or professional and technical associations.

22) Must fill out paperwork as required for tracking welding related and production characteristics

Physical requirements

- Adequate corrected vision required to perform work duties
- Must be able to lift 70 pounds
- Must be able to read English
- Must be have normal hearing

PPE required:

Hardhat, Safety Glasses, Hearing protection, Steel toe boots, gloves, occasionally leather sleeves, Welding Helmet, tinted cutting glasses, dust mask, respirator, fall protection, Hi tension equipment

---

Each job, with rare exception, is a difficult one with fresh challenges every day. Have you ever tried to take on someone else's responsibilities while they were on vacation? It's not easy, and there is often a moment when you find yourself mumbling, "My goodness, I had no idea they did all of this!"

Start with a job description and collect detailed input—and I mean *detailed!* As this happens, three wins emerge. First, you grow to better understand your team's role and the value they bring to the table. Second, it shows your team that you are invested in the process. And third, you know what you are looking for should the position need to be filled.

This is the starting point for understanding and gives you an idea for how to improve.

STEP 2: MEET REGULARLY

Robert Griggs

From: Robert Griggs [rgriggs@trinityinc.com]
Sent: Wednesday, August 05, 2009 10:30 AM
To: 'Bryan Davis'; 'Jim Nazzoli'; 'Ken Colletta'; 'Kristy Pride'; 'Phyllis MacConnell' 'Vince Hasen'
Subject: Management Meeting Agenda

Folks, please come prepared to discuss the standard items for your department & the issues you are bring up. Kristy will take minutes in Phyllis's.
Order of Reports
1- Discuss session plan. (Robert & Kristy) Review Minutes for last meeting
   - We need to discuss the guides lines for decision making. Exp
      - Cap X max $ spend per yr
      - Raises for people making over $ 40k must be approved team
      - Can't purchase anything over $ 10k with out team approval
      - Can't purchase inv. out side the inv. plan with out approval
      - Must have budget in place & measure against it ea Qt
         - We'll call this " Our Internal Convenience" What should they be?
Jim these are the same type of guide lines the Investor group has placed on us now. Let's discuss & give some thought. I'd like a rough draft by Sept 15th & them review for next meeting.

2- Purchasing & Scheduling / Bd
      - review inv. plan levels & is it correct?
      - Review sch back log
      - Discuss vendors
      - pricing What are ea mills base & extra charges?
      - Discuss short term goals from last meeting
      - 3Q short term goals
3- IT - Kp
      - Updates short terms goals from last meeting
      - General update on system
      - Keep minutes for meeting
4- Operation Ken
      - Discuss backlog
      - review downtime reports
      - review standards for On task % & No Repairs %
      - General update on project for Corp
      - Short terms goals & Q3 goals
5- Sales / Vh
      - Sales against budget by category
      - Discuss Qtly reviews with salesman / who do we like
      - List 75% target jobs for Q3 & 4
      - Discuss margins
      - QA /
      - Discuss Short terms goals
6- Finance Jim
      - review 1st 6 mo & Q3 forecast
      - Review margins, exp, credits, taxes deposits, convenience requirements, Bonus plan.
      - Review any other reports you feel are important.
      - Short term goals

7- Group Project
      - Want us to decide what the standard discussion point are for each category, at this meeting.

Thanks for your effort. This is how our company is going to be run & you are the people running it. I don't want you to hold anything back. Say what needs to be said.

During our weekly times together, we meet with groups doing the same job and ask basic questions such as the following:

- What would make your life better or easier?

- What tools, processes, or systems would help your department?

- Are there any procedure improvements you would recommend?

- What's not working for you, the customer, or the company?

This last one is particularly important, because your team members almost always know the answer. But the key is to make sure they feel safe to tell you the truth. This is a problem for most companies because despite what leaders might tell their teams, they have not created a safe place for those on their team to share their challenges and frustrations.

But this does not have to be you. Think about it: Wouldn't you like to be among the small percentage of companies in the world where honest conversations could take place?

As a leader and owner, you must have a thick skin! I like to say, "You can't hurt my feelings, because I have a lovely wife and wonderful kids who have that job!"

STEP 3: WRITE DOWN EVERY IDEA AND BREAK THEM INTO SIMILAR CATEGORIES

COSi PROJECTS	Start	STATUS / COMPLETE??	# Days
		CURRENT "COSI" PROJECTS:	
Job Submittal Checklist	Aug-2013	8/22 - Team met, developed checklist, BG submited examplein BD and VH for review. 8/29 - Met with BD, VH not yet. Think should be limited to written checklist on points to think about when giving a submittal, to be located in "required information for Salesman" agreed salesmen folder. BG has the working checklist, will work on hyperlinking to forms.	39
Payout - Write up procedure for inspection standards and train personnel on procedure for each criteria D1.1: (1) Visual Inspection, (2) Ultrasonic Inspection	Apr-2013	Requested by RG at 4/1/13 Mill Main Meeting ON HOLD UNTIL SHAWN B FREES UP PROJECTS 8/8 - RG said we want to say we have trained this person and that, on what to look for ("thumbnail") and what to do when they detect a defect. SB said will be figured out peramters for each size/diam/speed/wire. RG said can be as little as 6 things or something. SB said can do fairly quickly. RG wants taught 5 defects to payout and guys handle pipe thereafter, rick & guys on what to look at. Drew is now certified as an AWS level 2 UT written procedure for customers. 8/15 - SB need to pull things out of code book, have powerpoint with applicable. Steering Committee decided the groupd should officially "form" with goal, team, etc. Jim to iniiate. 8/22 - Jim to inform John N he is lead and what is entailed with being team lead. (old email 8/23) 8/29 - SB not here, John N said Paul making pwerpoint presentaion.	161
MILL PIPE CLASSIFICATION: Develop process & standards for classifying,as well as handling from payout to yard - Mill Pipe as PRIME STANDARD (Job or Inventory), PRIME NON-STANDARD, NON-CONFORMING, STARTER, & TRANSITION	Aug-2013	8/7 - This team may now evelove into a team that address need for a team as per RG's 8/5 email "Everyone I would like to meet to discuss this report. We need to set up a Cosi project to set standards for some of these items & then track to get better. Exp we produced 12 tons of 97.5 OD x .750 nonconforming – This cost $ 9000 & we loss $ 200 k this month, this can't happen. Total of 45 tons for month @ $ 750 - $ 33,750 this is just on Non-Conforming pipe, we really need to pick some of this cash up & put it in our pocket. 8/29 - Met Tuesday to develop process & standards for classifying - as well as handling from payout to yard - as PRIME (job or inventory), NON-STANDARD, NON-CONFORMING, STARTER, & TRANSITION Mill Pipe.). We have a stragy to handle current pipe the yard, as well as handle pipe made in each catagory going forward.	39
MILL PIPE PROFIT PER HOUR- Measure GP$/Hour. Set and Provide Job Run Standards to Mill, then Measure Actual and compare/analyze ON HOLD 8/23/13	Aug-2013		39
Salesmen Account Allocation	Aug-2013	8/8 - Working with KP pulling "unwanted" contacts out of a salesman's database, which will establish the pool of unassigned accounts, then next step is structure/process for reassigning these accounts. 8/15 - KP pulled out of the test data today, BD needs to rerun his process and make sure working thet way he intended, then move to doing for all salesmen, identify accounts to allocate, then process to allocate to salemen. 8/22 - He is making progress, got file from KP, RG/BD agreed MUST be done by 8/31 (JN e-mail reminder) 8/29 - Will run this weekend with August info, ready to move on to next step - (to work with Jim) RG said "I gotta know who we are NOT calling.	39
New/ALL employee/crown/contractors orientation - **start with safety.**	Aug-2013	6/13 - Safety Comm will discuss at next week and form a team 7/11 - KP/PM will inform SG/JW to meet with Jim to orientate on COSI and start of a team 7/18 - PM told JW7SG to see me and they wrote a note to do so 7/25 - emailed Jon, get with SG and meet me to discuss COSI process and being team lead. 8/15 - establish team, met with brainstorming, going over training videos position specific, coordinate with Crown what they wll do for us in the hiring. Making up a test form to make sure they know enogh to start (read a tape measure). Also gave each team member homework assignments. 8/22 - Met yesterday, establishing a list fro Crown, dos/don'ts, PPE list, still working on videos, other big thing, property checklist/procedure for leaving company (what to turn back in or inform Crown) 8/29 - Met yesterday, viewed tailers on orientation on safety/as well as job specific (crane operators, etc.), $195 for a package, unavailable (full, partial, exemption and why), MO audit thru 6/30, so BSW get us by 10/1 back. Discussed a visitor orientation with a sign-off, so they are an "approved" visitor (maybe for a year).	39
MO Use Tax Reporting/Tracking System and Procedure	Mar-2013	3/28 - First meeting scheduled for 4/1. MO 5/23 - BSW giving us a decision matrix for all items we buy listed as taxable, not taxable, etc. 6/5 - no update for this project from 5/23. Our comments have been sent back to BSW regarding the decision matrix and we are waiting for a budget number before we give them a go ahead. I will follow up soon as it is my understanding we need to have this in place by July 1st for use tax tracking. 6/13 - Followed up 6/12. Still waiting for budget 6/27 - BSW to deliver today the tax decision matrix for all purchases. 7/11 - Met with BSW last week. TDM proposed budget to be $7K - $10K. Includes itemized transaction study and backup for each tax decision along with training. 7/18 - accepted propasl via e-mail (AMY is our contact) working now to get TDM. 7/25 - Followed up with timeline, we said Oct 1 in place and us up to speed, so only on open quater 7/1-10/1 exposed, she said reasonable and shooting for sooner. First pass draft of matrix by Friday as well as answer questions from Eugene's prior first draft. 8/1 - BSW sent matrix draft just today, by catagory with examples, and taxability (full, partial, exemption and why), MO audit thru 6/30, so BSW get us by 10/1 8/5 - no update except respond we are good with the format 8/15 - no update, don't expect update until September, project should end by early October 8/22 - no update 8/29 - no update, don't expect until mid-September.	165
WPS Database	Mar-2013	3/28 - Just started Shawn to solidify the WPS database 5/23 - this is an ever evolving task , as our type of work always throws a new twist 6/6 - RG wants most common (S-8-10??) "typical", knowing we will ever be adding in the future 6/13 - Shawn will look and see what they have, get with John N and report back what we have 6/27 - On Hold with work schedule, looking what we have and how genericly it can cover our needs & gaps. Workingh to eliminate us "customizing" WPS for a job - get with Bryan D on what we buy in job folder and how will succeed with Salesmen 7/11 - NO MEETING 7/18 - SB to get w/ BD and John N and dicuss needs to identify what WPS cover majority and look for eficencies in how we document in job file. 7/25 - SB unavailable, 8/1 - Out in field, unavailable 8/8 - SB to write the S-6 or so +/-for the Mill and maybe 2 for Fab for basic weld to cover 99% of instances. RG wants SB to write these. SB said done by 9/15. 8/15 - needs to pass two for Products to John N then to sales guys, for Mill, will be based on COSI team generating rolling standards (Jim's) 8/22 - Met, Evan keeps mannual, want develop electronic detta base provided by Lincoln, this will dump to spreadsheet and maintain by job so we have for historical data.	165
ASME Spiral Pipe accepted for conveyance of gas and liquid	Mar-2013	3/28 - Something by July 5/23 - I have received info in regards to becoming an ASME certified shop / this will take some doing, as it requires an endorsement from a specialized insurance company, and state recognition, RG has help of secret santa 6/6 - Sectret Santa said certified within 4-6 weeks, may begin by end of year, RG to look into 6/13 - as get closer, RG will evaluate need, and cost, Santa said 30 days to do, only 7 companies with the "seal" - keep on radar 6/27 - Shawn has gotten tid-bits of info, still work ON HOLD Robert 8/1 - RG's next 6 month goal 8/15 & 8/22 - RG getting feet under him for a couple weeks	165

Organize, prioritize, and monetize every idea you receive so you have a strong list to work from moving forward. This step is critical. Nothing comes off the list until it has been completed or deemed not worthy of doing.

Again, this process demonstrates to your employees that you take their ideas seriously. It invites them into the conversation and provides you with the necessary information to make informed decisions. In the process, you build instant credibility that allows you to hold them accountable.

STEP 4: DEVELOP INCENTIVE PROGRAMS AROUND WHAT IS NOT WORKING

TRINITY 2021 PROFIT SHARING - UPDATE as of 10/28/21
*** YOU MUST BE EMPLOYED TO SHARE - YOU LEAVE YOU LOSE ***

		Net Profit	When and how much is paid each quarter?			
			Pay 4/30/21	Pay 8/6/21	Pay 11/12/21	Pay Mar/Apr '22
Quarter 1	January	$604,260	15%	15%	20%	50%
	February	$2,723,940				
	March	$1,149,213				
Quarter 2	April	$2,693,901		30%	20%	50%
	May	$3,845,672				
	June	$2,944,272				
Quarter 3	July	$1,760,428			50%	50%
	August	$1,619,097				
	September	$2,652,526				
Quarter 4	October	Not Yet				100%
	November	Not Yet				
	December	Not Yet				
Total Net Profit "SO FAR"!!		$19,993,309	<--TO DATE - SUBJECT TO CHANGE WITH FUTURE Profit/(Loss)!!			
SHARE 10% OF PROFITS!!		$1,999,331	<--TO DATE - SUBJECT TO CHANGE WITH FUTURE Profit/(Loss)!!			

	ESTIMATED PROFIT SHARING BASED ON NET PROFIT "SO FAR"...				
	Quarter 1	Quarter 2	Quarter 3	Quarter 4	TOTAL
	"Bucket" 1	"Bucket" 2	"Bucket" 3	"Bucket" 4	
% paid (less prior buckets)	15%	30%	50%	100%	
TOTAL	$69,551	$349,287	$580,828	$999,665	$1,999,331
NEW Estimate PER PERSON "SO FAR" -->	$440	$2,130	$3,542	$6,096	$12,207
WHEN DO WE PAY??	PAID 4/30/21	PAID 8/6/2021	11/12/2021	Mar/Apr 2022	
Increase due to September FINAL -->	$0	$0	$760	$760	$1,519

After collecting everyone's ideas, highlight those projects in your organization that are not moving forward. Then develop metrics that help you deal with these challenges and get the ball rolling again.

Often this involves laying down some serious cash on the table to incentivize your employees to do those hard tasks that no one wants to tackle. And when I say cash, I mean *cash*! Seriously, you will look like a cheap curmudgeon if you skimp on this step. Do not expect employees to care about a goal, metric, or incentive plan they did not help design, think is fair, and receive adequate compensation for.

At Trinity, we pick maybe one to three action items we want to improve upon per department, and the results are almost immediate. This process always moves the needle!

STEP 5: BUILD A SCOREBOARD

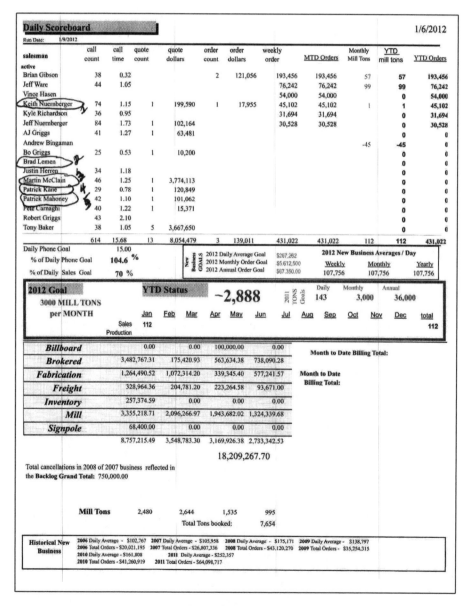

Early scoreboard from 2012

We use the scoreboard to measure our daily progress, post it for everyone to see, talk about ways we are hitting the mark or falling short, and then pay up!

A basic question every business owner should ask themselves is this: "Would I pay X dollars every week to get what I want?" If the answer is yes, your decision is obvious. Pay a little bit more, make a higher return in the process, fix a problem, and increase everyone's profit!

After this phase is complete, it's your job to fix these problems and do this same process all over again. You continue tracking the old metric and monitor its progress, but you find new areas of your company that are stagnant and tackle these fresh challenges. This is where persistence comes into play.

Remember, greatness and success happen in slow motion! What happens next is that people learn the process and start to enjoy getting better. They understand this makes their lives better and learn to enjoy the game, the money, and the challenge. Through this process, you are teaching them a system for success they can use forever in every aspect of their lives.

As this happens, you start to get more people thinking the way you think. They like the money, they want to be around people who know how to work, and they want to win! You start to build more loyalty and surround yourself with people who want to be on your team. And it is not long until you wake up and realize you have developed a winning culture.

Through this process, you are building and developing leaders. You develop a higher standard, and a culture of winning begins to take root in your organization. This allows the top of the org chart to focus on opportunities and growth.

Flip the Pyramid

I started using a phrase several years ago that has since caught on in our work community. It's called "flip the pyramid."

The bottom of the pyramid, not the top, should be what is most important, because it is there that employees do all the work. Upper management should work for these individuals instead of the other way around. After all, it is the wider portion of the pyramid that is client facing and bringing in your revenue.

The bottom of the pyramid—the widest part—is the foundation of your organization . Because I believe this, I try to model this mindset by example. Every six months, our mill needs to be cleaned. There is nothing glamorous about this task. But despite being in my midsixties, I make it a point to go down and be among my team, working on the dirtiest job in the process. And guess what? The team loves it. Why? Because it is a statement of my respect for them and what they do.

As I have witnessed firsthand, if we can make this group happy, improve their lives, and make their jobs easier, life gets better for everyone involved. When everyone on the team is happy, the customers are also happy.

Flipping the pyramid is not always easy and takes time, but it is doable! When I first met my friend Jack Stack, the godfather of open-book management, I looked at all the success he had experienced and said to him, "Jack, I don't think we can ever get to where you are at." He looked back at me and said, "Yes, you can. We are just ten years ahead of you on the journey."

> The mottoes and processes I outline in this book are simple to grasp but difficult to execute.

As it turned out, his prediction was right. The mottoes and processes I outline in this book are simple to grasp but difficult to execute. This is where discipline is needed to keep making the right choices every single day. It's recognizing that the foundation below the water is what is most important and investing all that you can into making sure that the foundation will last for generations.

Takeaways

➡ Successes happen in slow motion.

➡ List some ways you've met and gotten your team's input on processes or decisions. Start today!

➡ Here are some questions to ask:

   ▫ What's not working?

   ▫ What are we doing badly?

   ▫ What would make your, or your customers', lives easier?

➡ Think of ways you've been accountable to your team and list them out. How about ways that you've held them accountable?

➡ Think of a negative person that you've kept on the team and ask yourself why.

   ▫ Similarly, list any negative behaviors that you've seen and accepted.

➡ Do you think your team feels safe to tell you the truth at any moment? If not, why?

➡ Make a list at the end of each day of what you need to do first thing the next morning—and put the hardest one first!

➡ Make a list of people you think you could move higher in the organization. Write out a plan to have these people fill leadership positions and share it with your team.

➡ Think of ways you've served your employees and customers.

➡ Pick important metrics or standards that drive your business.

➡ Hold regular meetings to discuss your company's issues and goals.

    ▫ In these meetings, write down every question your team asks and every response to the questions above. Start working on addressing them as soon as possible!

➡ Incentives or even games could help address these issues as well as scoreboards to keep track.

➡ Last, think about ways to make your job *easier*. It won't get easier unless you are actively exploring ways to address it.

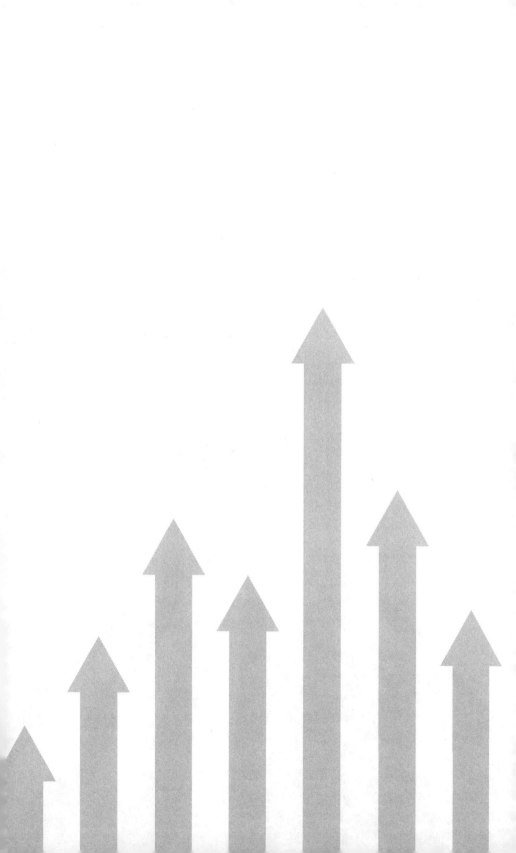

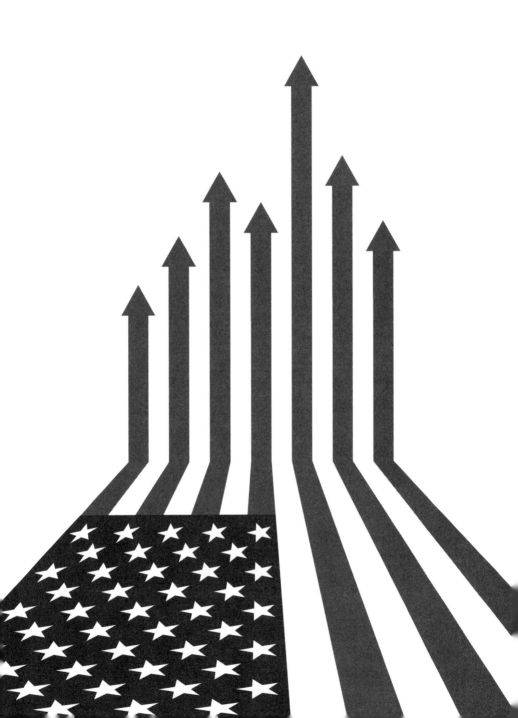

CHAPTER 4

LEAD WITH AN OPEN BOOK

Twenty years into Trinity's existence and our numbers continued to improve. Year after year, we grew. We worked hard and built infrastructure. All areas of our business were starting to mature. Still, something was missing.

Even though we had been in business for years, I still didn't feel like we'd made it. While I couldn't put my finger on it, I knew we were not all pulling in the same direction. Work felt harder than it should have been. When your team has the correct goals and vision, there is flow and continuity. You might be working harder than ever, but the process feels calmer and easier.

Despite being profitable, I could tell there was a big difference between earning a living and really making a profit. We were making progress, but we were not making real money—the kind of money that allows you to grow, prosper, and properly invest in yourself.

House money, as I call it, gives you freedom to hire for the future and invest for the next product line that gets you to the next plateau. We didn't have this. Instead, we were always playing with my "chips." While I didn't mind reinvesting my proceeds in the business, doing so was always a bit scary, and I knew there must be a better way that would free me from the pressure I felt every night.

Around this time, I noticed there was this dad at my kids' school who seemed to have his act together. He didn't have the slick presence of some businesspeople I knew, but from all appearances he knew what he was doing.

One afternoon as our kids practiced soccer together, my curiosity got the better of me, and I asked him how he became so successful. He invited me to his office to talk business, and during our conversation he handed me Jack Stack's *The Great Game of Business*.

My friend went on to explain what he called open-book management. This meant everyone in his company knew the financial numbers and shared in the profits. As a result, they not only shared in the numbers but shared in responsibility. There was incentive to do their jobs and do them well.

Something about this approach rang true. I went home with the book and read it immediately. I could tell this was who I was and how I wanted to run my business. *Share the profits and share the responsibility.* I liked the sound of that, and it just made so much sense.

The next day I approached my business partner Vince, who owned 17 percent of our company, and told him about this new way of doing business. I gave him a copy of the book, and after he read it, we ran over some of the mutual concerns we shared and soon made the decision to move forward. In my mind we had nothing to lose.

That decision proved to be one of the greatest steps we ever took.

The Shift from Managers to Leaders

This topic of open-book management raises the subject of leadership. Personally, I prefer the term *open-book leadership*. It's taking Robert Greenleaf's concept of servant leadership (referenced in the previous chapter) and remembering that the more you give, the more you receive. It's being fully transparent.

The ideals of leadership have shifted over the decades. With the dawn of the industrial age and assembly lines, we had managers who oversaw their teams. In the previous chapter I mentioned Andrew Carnegie's involvement in the Eads Bridge. What I did not mention was the horrible working conditions that existed in some of his factories. Everything was focused on the bottom line. The Carnegie Steel Company in Pittsburgh scarcely paid its workers a livable wage.

Henry Frick was the man in charge. You might remember the uproar that took place with the infamous Homestead Strike. The workers protested their working conditions, and Frick got mad and called in a group of guards, armed to the teeth. As a result, many of the workers lost their lives.

But this was the fate of employees in the late nineteenth century. Railroads were built on the backs of Chinese labor. Working conditions in the mines were deadly. It was not unrealistic to think your job might cost you your life.

This began to change when guys like Henry Ford came along. Ford not only emphasized the importance of production lines for his Model Ts but also elevated the roles and working conditions of his employees. This was a game changer. The voices of employees were finally starting to be heard.

As the twentieth century progressed, a change took place—one that shifted from management to leadership. Take a quick scan of books written a few decades ago, and it's all management stuff. The goal was to get the most out of your teams in the most efficient manner possible.

But with the arrival of authors like Greenleaf, this tide began to turn. Part of this was due to the way society began to shift. As more and more marginalized people overcame discrimination and unions evolved, the common man and woman suddenly found themselves with a voice. People no longer accepted being told what to do. They wanted to be involved and appreciated—to have some skin in the game.

Managers became leaders. It was not enough to simply tell people what to do, put systems in place, and expect them to work for minimum wage. Employees wanted to have a seat at the table and have pathways to promotion.

I should point out that some chief executive officers (CEOs) handled this evolution poorly and almost created an environment where no one is in charge. The result has not been empowerment, but confusion. This is why balance is so important. Someone must be in charge and call the shots, but this should not be done in some dictatorial fashion and should be conducted through the lens of servant leadership.

While many buy into this open-book leadership philosophy today, this was not always the case. In fact, there are many in the past and present who are skeptical of the role leaders play in organizations. Some question its validity altogether.

Consider the author Jim Collins. I've taken our entire team through his book *Good to Great*. And as I worked on this chapter, I came across an article by Christine Lagorio-Chafkin. It was titled "Jim Collins Didn't Think Leadership Was Important to a Company's Success. Here's Why He Changed His Mind." In this piece, Collins talked about the time he was doing research for *Good to Great* and made this fascinating admission: "I was dubious of anything having to do with 'leadership.' I had long believed that if you observe a successful company over time, you find its success is not the result of a single leader."[8]

But when Collins shared this with his team, they pushed back. "They told me that, in studying the inflections of companies that went from 'good' to 'great,' it was clear the leader played a big role. I said, 'Well, let's go to our comparison companies that didn't make it. Some have towering, charismatic leadership but didn't make that good-to-great leap. Leadership is an irrelevant variable.'"

Once again, his team pushed back and demonstrated that a leader's ambition played a key role in their success with the organization. This prompted Collins to rethink his position. "In the end, I'm happy to admit my team was right: Great leadership, in its many personality packages, matters a lot." And leadership doesn't have to be one big personality. It can be a team of leaders "speaking the same message," and it needs to be a team of leaders! I'm not sure you'll last with one voice!

John Maxwell often says everything rises and falls on leadership. I am prone to agree. At Trinity, our goal is to find these leaders and give them the tools to lead in their own way.

I've heard it said that "management is doing things right; leadership is doing the right things." Good managers create strong systems. Good leaders motivate and empower employees to action. And in today's environment, people want to do the right thing!

---

8   Christine Lagorio-Chafkin, "Jim Collins Didn't Think Leadership Was Important to a Company's Success. Here's Why He Changed His Mind," last modified June 3, 2021, https://apple.news/AmjHQ_vWaS1mh1lw1V87Hyw.

Show You're Not Cooking the Books

The foundation of all open-book leadership must be trust.

For many companies, employees do not trust their leadership and assume any numbers or reports they have do not contain the full story. Someone is cooking the books!

This is a major challenge every leader of a company faces. Most employees are prone to view their boss with a degree of suspicion. As tennis legend Arthur Ashe notes, "Trust has to be earned and should come only after the passage of time." All this goes back to my simple point in chapter 2: tell the truth. Only as you tell the truth and back up what you say do people trust you.

There is a Chinese proverb that says, "Tell me and I forget, teach me and I may remember, involve me and I learn." When you do the right things the right way, this teaches your team what telling the truth means.

After reading Jack Stack's book multiple times and giving it to our leadership to read, perhaps no other phrase impacted me as much as his concept of open-book management. As Jack writes, "Open-book management is the best way I know of to keep people focused on the important issues facing a company."[9] Open-book management is about letting each member of the company see the financial statements, know how much profit is coming in, and understand what it takes to survive.

The idea of leading an organization with each member knowing every financial number of our company was both terrifying and something that seemed right. On one hand, I was afraid because it

---

9   Jack Stack and Bo Burlingham, *The Great Game of Business, Expanded and Updated: The Only Sensible Way to Run a Company* (New York: Crown Publishing, 2013), 103.

felt too vulnerable. What would employees think if we came across hard times and our numbers were down? Would they be compelled to say they deserved higher wages or become afraid and leave?

The concept of open-book leadership was simple to comprehend, but having the guts to follow through was going to be the real test. Still, I could see the tremendous upside. Leading with an open book would encourage involvement and hopefully pull our team together.

In the words of Sabrina Horn, "Why not steer clear of fakery by taking to the path to real leadership, an authentic foundation, and enduring success?"[10]

Talking to the Team

Three months after I finished Jack's book, I held our first team meeting in January 2000 to outline our new approach. Everyone was there. We had truck drivers, welders, and salespeople all piled into one room.

Ten minutes before this meeting took place, I stuck my head into Vince's office and said, "Tell me why we are doing this, again!" He laughed and reminded me this was my bright idea.

Together we walked into the room to find our team waiting. For the next two hours I worked through every facet of our business, explaining in detail the ins and outs of what we did. As I spoke, I could tell some understood immediately, others were more skeptical, and then some just needed time to process this new approach.

The main thrust of my message was financial literacy. I wanted to educate my team on what it took to run a business. Contrary to what many thought, there was a large difference between sales and profit. Just because we were doing $20 to $30 million in sales a year, that did

---

10 Sabrina Horn, *Make It, Don't Fake It: Leading with Authenticity for Real Business Success* (Oakland, California: Berrett Koehler Publishers, 2021).

not mean we were a highly profitable company. I outlined the dozens of primary expenses we had that limited our ability to increase wages.

As I spoke, I saw more and more light bulbs turn on as people began to realize what this might mean for them and their families. By the end I felt like many of them were on board, and there was a growing sense of excitement in the room.

Sensing some still needed more time to process, I offered my reassurances. "Listen," I told everyone, "you've got nothing to lose with this new approach. I understand if you're skeptical. That's fine! But just don't get in the way of others who buy in and drink the Kool-Aid." From there, the culture began to change.

Each month, we met together, and I outlined our progress. And to some people's amazement, they realized the books were not cooked. Trinity was not making money hand over fist and allowing its employees to get by on scraps from the table. They also learned about these two partners called the US government and the State of Missouri that took a combined 42 percent of our profits. It was an eye-opening experience, and the more I shared, the more everyone realized what it took to run a company of our scale.

That day I realized open-book leadership was one of the greatest ways I could show my employees I valued them. This new approach shifted the hierarchical structure and gave everyone on our team, from welders to salespeople, a seat at the table. Individuals who might have previously thought they had little to contribute to our team's success now realized they were valuable.

They felt like a team

An Invitation to Share in the Profits

At first, a few members of my inner circle did not share my excitement. "Robert, these guys don't get it," they said. "What you're saying is just going in one ear and out the other." But I didn't buy that. Sure, some of the concepts were packaged differently from what many were used to hearing, but the ideas were nothing new.

In my mind, if anyone knows what it takes to run a home, they know what it takes to run a business. I explained to our team that each member of our group was already a business owner. They ran their households, paid bills, and took care of their needs. Anything left over went into their personal savings. This was profit, and each one of them knew how difficult this was to attain.

> If anyone knows what it takes to run a home, they know what it takes to run a business.

Jack Stack often uses a phrase pronounced "stop-gooter" to illustrate an employee's mindset. It stands for "Skip the praise—give us the raise."[11] This is what your team wants. They don't want you to merely give them words of affirmation (although this helps). Instead, they want you to put your money where your mouth is. If you truly believe in them, be willing to back it up with some cold, hard cash. This is what I did.

My approach to open-book leadership is to talk about everything. Rather than hold back and take it slow, I immersed my team in every facet of the business—scheduling, building standards, quality control, you name it.

---

11   Jack Stack and Bo Burlingham, *The Great Game of Business, Expanded and Updated: The Only Sensible Way to Run a Company* (New York: Crown Publishing, 2013), 158.

Through our many conversations with all the leaders, we picked a critical number we knew would allow us to turn a profit. We discovered that 3.5 percent net return on sales was what it took to run our business. Consequently, this meant that anything short of this meant we could not pay out a dime in profit sharing at the end of the year. And in those years that we exceeded 5 percent in net returns, we gave 20 percent of the profit to members of our team.

Not only did these goals motivate members of my team, but they also motivated me. My goal was to engage every person on our team. I wanted them to recognize that the company's success determined their success. When we won as a group, we all won individually. All they needed to do was invest some time and energy and stay focused on the daily task of serving the customer—their boss.

This would lead to greater profits for all.

Learning Together

Because I engaged members of our team early in the process, they felt as though they were part of the team from the start. We were able to learn together as we went along. My uncertainty worked as a positive because it encouraged others to take initiative. It wasn't a "Hey, guys, Robert has this all figured out and I need you to get on board" situation. Instead, it was more of a collaboration. No one knew exactly what we needed to do or how to start. I just knew this was the direction we were headed.

My first action step was to sign our leadership group up for *The Great Game of Business* class with Jack Stack. The person who came down to lead this group was Bill Fotsch. After a few weeks, Bill and his team drove down, and we worked through his class for two days. This taught us the foundation of leading with an open book.

This process was both exhilarating and sobering. More than once I thought to myself, *What have I gotten us into?* We were excited about where this new direction might lead, but we also realized the monumental task of getting all folks rowing in the same direction. Personally, I felt the burden of responsibility land on my shoulders. I saw how difficult it was to run a business.

It was an eye-opener. This process taught me that all the insecurities I felt were justified. On my own, I wasn't smart enough and didn't have enough time to do what needed to be done. I had to have a team, and we had to work together.

Our Plan

Open-book leadership looks different for every person, but the basic principles remain the same. Looking back, I present here several pillars that shaped our success in this area.

PILLAR 1: SHARE THE PROFIT, SHARE THE RESPONSIBILITY

I was clear with our team from the start. Yes, there is tremendous upside for employees who engage, but in exchange for this upside, I required a greater level of accountability. Now it was not about Robert carrying the weight of the company on his shoulders. It was about all of us lifting together.

This went over like a lead balloon for some. To a few managers, this sounded like a lot of extra work. "This job is hard enough!" I heard some say. "I didn't sign up for this. Now I have to add more work to an already busy schedule."

While this process was uncomfortable as I responded to these new concerns, it was also where the rubber met the road. It told me who was in and who was out. I saw who I could depend on and who was just along for the ride. Some of the folks I thought were my greatest team players faltered, while some unlikely faces began to emerge.

Sharing the profit is an easy sell. Sharing the responsibility is a bit tougher.

PILLAR 2: BE VULNERABLE AND TRANSPARENT

The moment I decided on this new course for our company, I felt like the emperor who had no clothes. I was naked and exposed. All the secrets of our company were revealed, and this was very uncomfortable.

My insecurities plagued me as I imagined what my team must be saying behind my back. "Robert doesn't know how to run a company. If he did, we would be much more profitable than we are today! Maybe I am at the wrong place. Perhaps I need a change in career."

Tough as this was, I realized that if I wanted my managers and employees to be honest, I had to lead the way.

PILLAR 3: STAY COMMITTED

The temptation to give up and quit can be strong. In the first few days, the energy is great, and excitement is through the roof. But then it begins to cool, and reality sets in. There is this feeling of "My goodness, what have we got ourselves into?"

It's a bit like tackling that hundred-mile bike ride you've thought about doing for months. Everything about the idea seemed great in your mind, but sixty miles in you hit a mental wall. You start thinking to yourself, *This is ridiculous. I can't make it. Why did I even try?*

There were so many challenges that arose and tried to pull us off track. Employees didn't get on board, and this was frustrating. We would miss our initial projections because we weren't good at setting realistic goals, and this made all of us wonder if this would work.

When these thoughts first started to come, I felt isolated and as though I were the only person in the world with these struggles. The truth is that every great leader deals with voices like this that tell them to give up. Everything is easy when the economy, business, or life is good. But life has a way of taking us through more valleys than peaks.

This is a major lesson every entrepreneur needs to learn. Keep an even keel. Don't get too high in the good times, and don't get too down in the dumps in the bad.

Stay committed. Stay persistent!

PILLAR 4: DO NOT COMPROMISE STANDARDS

Part of open-book leadership was having our team set goals. We will get into this more in the next chapter with benchmarking, but it is critical to hold to the goals you set.

Yes, there might be times you adjust, but you need to hold fast to your goals. If you set a number to hit as a team and miss it by a small margin, it does not help your cause to adjust the goalposts and allow it to slide.

Once, around five years ago, our metrics on welding numbers on sign poles and a few other items started to drop. Because we have different degrees of welding, I assumed we were just in a season of difficult welding. But this period lasted longer than it should have, and I knew something was wrong.

After some research and meeting with everyone on the team, I found out one of our machines, the burn table, had a flaw and produced a larger-than-normal gap on our parts that resulted in longer manufacturing times. We did some tinkering, but the table was around twenty years old and had seen better days. Biting the financial bullet, we purchased a new table that cost us $120,000. While this initial bill was more than we anticipated, our parts got better, and we returned to our previous welding standards.

This provided a valuable reminder: it is never acceptable to create inferior products, so never compromise your standards.

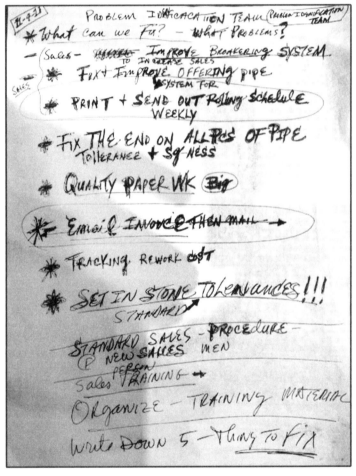

Original meeting list from our first COSI meeting PIT team on November 9, 2011

PILLAR 5: ELIMINATE EXCUSES

After asking our team to make a commitment to these new goals, I felt it was my obligation to do whatever I could to help them succeed. For me, this meant listening and hearing ways we could improve. I did not want us missing goals if there were simple fixes we could implement to keep us on track.

So, for starters, we gave every employee in the company a physical way to get better by meeting and discussing what wasn't working. It was a process, and we taught them every week how to improve. This is where everything started to tie together. These meetings and questions became the physical building blocks for how we improved.

Next I met with every division of our company. On Mondays I would meet with all ten of our welders and hand out sticky notes to collect feedback. From right to left, I asked each member for ways I could make their jobs easier. What could I do to eliminate the barriers that were making it tougher to achieve our mutually agreed-upon goals?

I was amazed at how practical and useful these sessions proved to be. One worker would say, "I need my welders running better." Another would chime in, "I need my work in front of me faster." Some weeks I'd collect upward of twenty suggestions.

Then, after I stepped out of these meetings, we on the leadership team would do whatever we could to fix whatever challenge they presented. Sometimes these were simple and involved a quick repair. Other times they were more complex. But they never came off our list till they were fixed or deemed not worthwhile. As we removed barriers, accountability on our team skyrocketed. There were fewer and fewer reasons for someone to offer why they had missed the mark.

Before long we started to hit our schedule every week. As we did, our numbers rose.

PILLAR 6: ALWAYS GET BETTER

Stagnation kills momentum. The moment you stop improving is the moment you start going backward.

I will cover this more in chapter 7, but the whole idea of continuous improvement must be baked into the open-book leadership process. The reason you share information is so your processes can improve and you can do more with less effort.

This idea of CI (continuous improvement) is a way of living for me. I incorporate it into everything I do.

PILLAR 7: KEEP THE RIGHT PEOPLE

Some employees looked at this open-book leadership philosophy and thought it was dumb. Their reaction was "This is stupid. Just tell me what to do and give me a raise."

This mindset told me much about who they were. Unless they changed, I could tell they would not be a fit on our team. I wasn't interested in having people on my team who clocked in and clocked out. If I was sharing the profits, I wanted them all in.

It was important they bought into our philosophy and realized their effort determined their pay and our future. If they worked hard, their income would continue to rise. I wasn't about to pay extra to people who weren't pulling their weight. I was OK with employees' skepticism. However, if those skeptics became disgruntled or negative, that was an issue.

> I wasn't interested in having people on my team who clocked in and clocked out. If I was sharing the profits, I wanted them all in.

Sometimes I stand back in amazement at the incredible team I have around me. I think back several years ago to a specific example. My wife and I were out for a drive on a nice Sunday afternoon when we happened to drive by the pipe mill. I noticed the gate was open, and there was a van parked in front of the office.

Curious, I pulled in, and after walking through the door, I noticed kids laughing and hanging out in the entry area. They told me their dad was in the shop. I walked back and found one of my key leaders unloading one of the railcars that holds steel coils to make pipe.

"Drew, what are you doing here?" I asked.

He explained his team needed the coils to run first thing at five o'clock the next morning, and he didn't want us to have to wait to load before we started the mill. So here he was on a Sunday afternoon, taking time to get everything set up.

I thanked him and returned to my wife in the car. Driving home, I was grateful for his commitment. The next day, I was curious and checked Drew's time card. He hadn't even clocked in for the day before. This told me a whole lot about him, and, unsurprisingly, he continues to remain a strong part of our team.

I'll keep guys like that around forever!

The Leadership Problem

The other day I was reading an article by David Finkel titled, "The Most Common Leadership Weaknesses I've Seen Over Twenty-Five Years of Business Coaching."

Fascinated, I started reading and paused when Finkel got to this list of leadership weaknesses. In his words, you struggle as a leader because:[12]

- You lack <u>a clear vision</u>, goals, and big picture strategy for your company, department, or team.

- Your team doesn't understand your vision, goals, or strategy. You may have them, but they haven't been clearly and effectively communicated to your entire team. This causes a lack of coherence and inefficiencies in your business as people and departments work out of phase.

- You have one or more <u>habitual behaviors that undercut your performance</u> as a leader.

- You have a hard time <u>letting go of control</u>. You've been burned so many times in the past that you tend to just do things yourself.

- Your company lacks leadership attention. If only you had more leaders, you could seize so many more of the abundant opportunities to grow your business.

- You avoid <u>tough conversations and confrontation</u>. Or you dive into these situations, but you don't do it tactfully or well.

- Your team has an attitude problem. They know what to do, but for whatever reason (e.g., a bad apple, lack of motivation, etc.) they just don't perform as they should.

- Your team misperceives you. They interpret your behaviors and communications in negative ways.

---

12 David Finkel, "The Most Common Leadership Weaknesses I've Seen Over Twenty-Five Years of Business Coaching," accessed January 19, 2022, https://www.inc.com/david-finkel/the-most-common-leadership-weaknesses-ive-seen-over-25-years-of-business-coaching.html.

- Your team isn't accountable. <u>They miss deadlines or drop balls</u>. Avoidable mistakes have cost you greatly. You've lost customers. You've been put in embarrassing situations having to fix things.

- Everyone you manage keeps coming back to you to get your input. At times, it feels like you're doing your job plus a lot of other people's jobs.

- Your current managers just haven't matured yet as leaders. They want to do a good job but lack the skills and experience to be great managers right now.

Notice that all of these are within the leader's control. It does not take someone who is highly gifted to do many of these well. It's important things like knowing where you want to go, communicating with clarity, having conversations others won't have, and holding people accountable to do what they said they would do.

When you do these simple things well, everything else begins to fall into place. But when you neglect these areas, you fall into trouble. From my observation, Finkel's list highlights the common flaws I notice in leaders every day. But when you flip the script, allow others to point out your areas you need to improve, and commit yourself to being transparent with others, great things can happen.

What Do You Have to Lose?

If you have drawbacks to the open-book leadership approach, my question for you is this: *What do you have to lose?* The answer is nothing! The moment I started open-book leadership was the moment I felt the power of all the people involved. I felt energy from everyone on my team.

Back in those first few days of implementation, I remember talking to Jack Stack and telling him there was no way we would ever arrive at where he was at. He smiled and said, "Sure you will. We've just had a twenty-year head start!" Rewind ten years and there is no way I could have envisioned who we have become today. But Jack's projection proved accurate.

It's a terrible feeling to have the weight of your whole business on your shoulders, but it is a fantastic feeling to have the power of all your employees and partners behind you. It makes you feel invincible and like nothing can stop you.

Takeaways

➡ "Management is doing things right; leadership is doing the right things."—Peter Drucker

➡ How willing are you to be transparent with your team? What types of information would you open up (sales, expense budgets, etc.)? On the other hand, list out any information that "scares you" should it be available to all employees and ask yourself, "Why?"

➡ Think about your budget. Do you keep track of it daily? Monthly? If not, why aren't you?

➡ A very small percentage of companies have a list of standards for their business (or for each department). If you don't have one yet, get started now!

➡ Document processes and procedures for the most important functions you do at your company.

➡ List all the employees and vendors that go above and beyond for your company and share it with the team.

➡ Rank your biggest weaknesses and tackle them one by one, starting at the top. Similarly, you should rank your strengths and never lose sight of them.

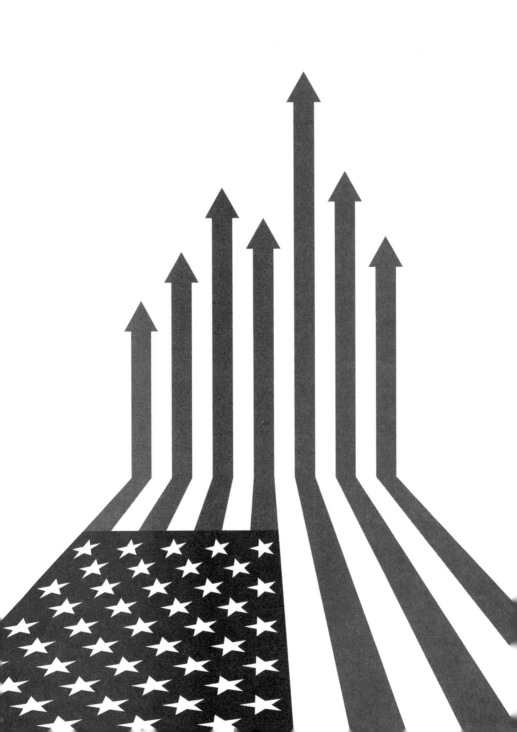

CHAPTER 5

SET THE BENCHMARK

Shifting to open-book leadership made everyone, myself included, a bit nervous.

Some of our team thought this new system might be used as a tool against them. They worried it could result in getting them to do more work with less compensation or be used as leverage to cut their pay.

Sensing this, I made certain to have numerous conversations to make sure we were all on the same page. I reassured them this was in fact a win for everybody, and before long we were all in agreement. Their confidence started to build as they understood hard workers would be recognized and compensated accordingly, while those who fell behind would receive coaching. To the great employee this would be a godsend. It would prove their worth and superiority, making accountability their friend.

This accountability came through benchmarking.

It is important to pick a critical number to schedule the week and process around accordingly. This is what benchmarking is. Just as a good weightlifter knows how many repetitions they need to do each day to grow their muscles, an organization must know what it needs to do to grow its business and make it more efficient and stronger. It's looking at what the best in your industry are doing and then doing your best to match and eventually rise above them.

Through effective benchmarking, our goal was to get our product on time to our customer at least 95 percent of the time. This might seem low, but we have a complicated product that takes months to produce with many different details, and we wanted to make sure we were realistic. Then, on those few instances we fell short, we would either offer overtime to our team to make sure there were no more delays, or we would communicate with the customer and let them know the revisions to the schedule.

Benchmarking is a triple win. It keeps employees on pace so they can receive incentive payments, it benefits management because it allows them to see where they need to improve, and it keeps customers happy with on-time delivery. The communication moving in all directions keeps the systems fluid and helps morale because everyone is in the know.

The Budget Is the Starting Point

Effective benchmarking is impossible without a clear budget. If you don't have a budget, you don't have anything. I would argue you don't even have a company. You might think you do, but you don't.

Jack Stack says, "In my experience, most people approach budgeting with a mixture of cynicism and boredom. At best, they regard it as a meaningless exercise in which they feed back to top management the numbers it wants to hear. Alternatively, they feel they are being forced to help design the club they are going to be beaten over the head with for the next twelve months. Almost no one views budgets as tools for increasing productivity or making money."[13] Budgeting, when it's done right, is the vehicle to drive success, communication, involvement, and lots of wins. It is the map to success.

Any leader who takes on the responsibility of keeping others employed owes it to their team to have a written budget that measures their progress. It is the only way you can hold yourself and your team accountable. Without this, no one knows the score of the game, and you cannot tell if you're winning or losing.

> Any leader who takes on the responsibility of keeping others employed owes it to their team to have a written budget that measures their progress.

Over time, I realized that building a budget is a great way to establish trust with your team and keep the wolves away from the door. Banks and vendors appreciate it when you can project the future accurately. Whenever I realize we are about to get tight, I call one of our partners and say, "Hey, just a heads-up, but it looks like we are going to miss our numbers this quarter. If you want to grab lunch to talk about it, let me know."

I've always made it a point to underpromise and overdeliver to my bank. In my opinion, it's better to undersell yourself a bit than it is to say you're sorry you missed the projection. Because Trinity's growth has continued for several decades, my relationship with the bank has been our cash lifeline. This meant it was essential to have a relationship built on trust.

---

13 Jack Stack and Bo Burlingham, *The Great Game of Business, Expanded and Updated: The Only Sensible Way to Run a Company* (New York: Crown Publishing, 2013), 188.

It's amazing how this strengthens relationships. I've taught our team it is a sign of strength to know what is coming down the road and to ask for help when a challenge arises. Think about this for a second. Imagine if all the people who reported to you gave you a heads-up whenever a challenge arose. Wouldn't you trust them more?

Budgeting has a twofold purpose. It lets you know where you are, and it helps those around you trust your decision-making.

A budget is a living, breathing document that contains your best estimates. Sometimes they are accurate; other times they need to be adjusted when things change. There have been times we have set a budget and realized we were well off the mark. In these moments, we do a deep-dive assessment and get back on target. The more you do them, the better you get. It is only through many failures that we can have the accurate budgets we do today.

How to Create a Budget

Initially, our Trinity team set three budgets. The first was our *bank budget*. It was more conservative, and it was a number we could hit in our sleep. The second was our *normal budget* that was right down the middle. It was our most accurate projection but did not consider outside factors that might contribute to added success or failure, like a natural disaster or war or stock market crash. Then there was our *stretch budget*. This is what we hoped to hit, and it stretched us to become better and shoot for more. This is the outcome that we threw a party for at the end of the year when things went our way!

While doing three budgets might sound like a lot of work, I can assure you it isn't. When I design budgets with my teams, I don't over-complicate the process. Essentially I just make sure the bank budget is a can't miss, the normal budget is reasonable, and the stretch budget reflects where our team would like to be if the chips fall our way. That's it. Very simple.

Today our team works off the normal budget. Each October, every salesperson submits a sales number by category and customer. They also include targeted customers they haven't sold before but are planning to close. In addition, we bring in members from every department, in each category or line item for the income statement, and collect their input. This includes employees from the shop, office, and sales.

Then we work down the income statement and discuss the various line items from past years' information and sales figures that are needed to hit our budget. Since we've already benchmarked the sales category, we have the vital information to set the budget expense numbers.

This forces our sales team to look at their individual book of business and make a commitment to the team, themselves, and the company as to what they are going to do. From there, they meet monthly with our sales manager to see how things are progressing. This process built accountability into our system and allowed our shops to forecast how much labor was needed.

Again, I think of a budget as the road map to the future. It is the syllabus for success. Yes, sometimes things need to change, but without a budget and clear plan of action, you are preparing yourself for failure. With a budget, every time you miss a projection, you can go back, evaluate, and ask the important questions. *Why did we miss? What do we need to do to get back on track?*

Unfortunately, this step seems so basic to some that they feel free to neglect it. "Budget, right," they say to themselves. "I know I'm supposed to have one. But who has time for this?" Smaller companies might say to themselves, "Do we really need a budget at our stage?"

My unequivocal response is yes! Without one, your company is sunk before it sets out to sea.

It saddens me that many high schools and universities don't do a better job helping students understand the basics of budgeting. But as we have taught financial literacy or basic budgeting to members of our team, it's amazing how this has transformed their thinking. It's caused many to rethink the way they budget at home.

As we worked our way through open-book leadership, we taught our team how a company should be run. They learned there is profit and loss. Not all months are the same and not all times of the year are the same. They begin to see how much business can fluctuate from day to day and see the many peaks and valleys.

And as we developed the expense side, everyone got involved. This is the whole point of leading with an open book. As everyone reviews the budget together, there becomes more and more collective interest in the mission. The teams see how we can make a profit, share with others, and have fun in the process! Before long, it becomes a game where you are trying to predict the outcome.

While I know talking about budgets can cause some people's eyes to roll back in their sockets, I cannot overemphasize how enjoyable it can be if you do some of the grunt work on the front end. Because we laid a strong foundation of budgeting at Trinity, each month continues to get easier with more repetitions. Today budgeting is second nature.

The budget is the foundation for continuous improvement. As you improve, you get better and better. The better you get, the more addictive and fun this becomes for the team.

Create Collective Buy-In

In our first meeting, we got everyone in the room and put our company budget on the big screen. This was different from the past.

Before, only a few managers saw the budget or had a say in creating it. As a result, we had a team of people who were disconnected from the budget, and there was little buy-in. But when we brought everyone together, this changed.

This was when it got serious. Everyone could see what we were making. But to me this step was critical, because I couldn't ask people to buy into a system to which they were not committed. I wanted to dispel the myth that the company always made the lion's share of the profit while the workers received almost nothing for their efforts.

So together we went over every line item in our budget. I shared exactly what it took to run the business, and I invited their input. I wanted them to share ways we could improve. *How could we make a profit? How could we come in below budget?*

For example, take our sales with sign poles. We brought both the salespeople and those who worked on the poles together. This helped us not only from a budget standpoint, but it also instilled some team camaraderie. Both sides grew to understand the entire process. The salespeople realized what it took to make the poles, and the workers understood the challenges of selling.

We literally did this for every expense category. I would bring someone from sales and the shop to work on every item. On more complicated matters, such as insurance, I invited someone from accounting into the conversation. Salaries and labor costs were a lump number that only our controller and CFO reviewed with department managers.

Initially, these hour-long meetings occurred twice a week for three to four weeks so that we could get all the information and know each step of the budgeting process. After we observed trends and patterns for a few months, we came up with a new budget line item that served as a fresh and more accurate starting point. Yes, this was slower, but it gave us total buy-in on the budget moving forward.

When our larger team met for our monthly finance meeting, there would be a person from each group who presented their line item number. Then, if there was any sort of variance, they were asked to explain. This proved to be an excellent way to find leaders. As I have discovered, some people are born to lead. Unfortunately, sometimes they do not get the opportunity. But this process gave people a chance to step up.

To the ones who just wanted a raise without the accountability, they found Trinity was not the place for them. But for those who were quiet but looking for an opportunity to step up, this proved to be just the opportunity they wanted.

This also led us to understand why and how we needed to pick our critical numbers or benchmarks. In the budget these benchmarks are what drives the success of every process and budget. For example, when we first got started with this process, we didn't even know that something as basic as the flux-to-wire ratio was something to track! But after one of our welding experts sat in on a meeting, he made us second-guess our decision, and we realized how much money we could save by keeping track. I could repeat this same type of conversation hundreds of times.

Creating collective buy-in was a process where we all learned together and gained a fresh appreciation for that old saying, "Knowledge is king." I have found that when we lay a foundation of solid budgeting and our team buys into the process, our leaders are able to get out in front of our company's challenges and lead at a higher level.

Creating a Culture of Accountability

The early days of Trinity's open-book leadership started with a simple whiteboard at the front of the room. Our great receptionist, Joan, would take down the numbers sold each day, put them in a spreadsheet, and then write them on the board each morning.

Everyone walked by the board, and it wasn't long before workers started to treat it seriously. If our sales team went three days without making a sale, everyone was on edge, and we knew something was wrong.

At the start of every day, we instituted a fifteen-minute huddle for most departments. Salespeople were asked what they were closing that day, and production workers discussed the schedule and status of ongoing and upcoming projects. We took these meetings seriously and made sure everyone was on time. This started each day on a proper note. Sure, we still had to do some babysitting and push some people to meet their goals, but this clear form of accountability kept everyone focused. Everyone knew what their standing was in the company, and this was very important.

Eventually we did away with the whiteboard and moved to a more sophisticated system: an emailed spreadsheet. Now our weekly sales numbers are sent out to all employees with a list of which salespeople are selling what along with profit margins. It's the same principle of accountability, but more detailed. We use a CRM software that allows us to rate every quote we give a customer. This way we know if the salesperson is just making a basic quote or if there is a high probability they will get the order. This allows our sales folks to make accurate predictions about what will happen.

It also forces our salespeople to get off the fence. Either they are or they aren't going to get the sale. It's accountability. This process tests them on their ability to know their customers and the situations they are quoting. If they do not get the job, why? *Who did get the job? What could they improve to make a better quote the next time?* These are the questions they will need to answer along with their other team members each Friday.

Every Friday, each member of my sales team, and sometimes other departments, joins a Friday-morning sales call where we run over the numbers. These meetings are direct, and we get down to business in a hurry. After sharing the broader picture of where we're at as a company, each salesperson gives us a brief report on their progress. This process builds in instant accountability for each salesperson to themselves, the team, and the company. As I remind them, without sales there are no accountants, shop people, IT, or HR. Everything rides on their success.

Together, we review and discuss which jobs we're going to close or other projects that are out in the marketplace. This meeting tells us how we should feel about current sales and what our next several months might look like. It's the gauge as to what is going to happen and helps us see where we are going. It's all about building a system through trial and error until it runs in such a way that everyone can sleep well at night.

It's all about accountability. I want to know what everyone on our team is thinking. No one is disconnected. We are all working together to pull our weight. Some on the team have more success than others, but we do what we can to help the others because it's our job to lift everyone up.

Picking the Critical Number

The next step is picking the critical number.

What is driving our sales? What is driving our machine uptime? What is driving our profitability? These are questions we ask ourselves all the time, and every member of our team must answer them. Is it our number of calls to customers or number of actual conversations? Is it the number of quotes we send out, or is it the number of people who actually give purchase orders off these quotes?

What is the secret formula that drives this business? Often it is a combination of things, but it helps if we narrow it down to a few factors. Sometimes these factors change, and that's OK. It's knowledge that is critical. If you don't know what moves the needle, you don't know what to shoot for every day.

When we first attempted to pick our company's critical number, we did some digging. We went to our bank and discovered through some research that the best companies close to our industry were making 5 percent net return on sales. To stay afloat, I knew we had to do a minimum of 3.5 percent to cover operating expenses and fund expansion. At the time, we were doing well and hitting around $20 million in annual sales. Dividing this by fifty-two weeks out of the year, and then by five days out of the workweek, meant we had to take in just shy of $77,000 a day at our budgeted margins to make a profit. So that became our benchmark or critical number—$77,000 in sales per day every day. If we hit or exceeded this number, we could afford to share profits with our team.

Now that $20 million in sales we used to make in a year takes us only a month in 2021. This means our numbers have shifted, but our goal of 3.5 percent net return on sales remains. In recent years, we have consistently exceeded this number, and this means there is more to go around.

When we picked our critical number as a company, it was important to share this number with our team and help them see where their department fit the larger picture. At the close of 2021, we had profit sharing of $13,541 per person. Granted, this was our best year ever, but who wouldn't want to work at a company that paid $13,541 in a year for profit sharing—even if it only happened occasionally?

Post the Number So Everyone Knows

Because everyone knows what our critical number is and has helped determine it, we know what we need to hit each day to move the needle. The number is the manager, which means you're now free to truly embrace being a leader. We know what we must do and how hard we must work to make it happen. Everything is tracked, not just in sales, but also in our shop.

In welding we expect each man to weld twenty feet an hour. It's what they agree to hit when they sign up for the job. We've already crunched the numbers and know it is doable. We expect them to stay on task 80 percent of the time and weld 160 feet a day. This is the benchmark, or critical number, for their department. It's a clear expectation that gets published daily and weekly. If one of the welders starts to fall short of this goal, we have a conversation and coach them to get back on track. And for those who exceed this goal, they help to make sure the monthly incentive bonus is hit and compensated accordingly.

> The number is the manager, which means you're now free to truly embrace being a leader.

To this point, here is a fun story to add. One of our largest suppliers nationally had a shop in St. Louis and hired one of our welders. My contact heard about it and called me to apologize, saying it would never happen again. I said, "Tom, I know, but do you know how many feet of welding this guy does a day?" He didn't. That's when I said, "I'm glad your guys hired him, because he only welds twelve feet an hour per day, and he was about to get fired!" We both laughed about it, but the larger point needs to be made. This is what happens when you have standards and benchmarks. People know when they need to move on!

Life is a competition. When we post the welding numbers daily, those who have the biggest numbers know where they are, and the rest of the team knows who they need to chase. If you have facts about the best welders, you know who to pay more. If someone asks me for a raise, I tell them to increase their rate, become more versatile, learn other skills, or ask to be cross-trained. This is how you become more valuable.

We also meet with each person from the shop every six months for a review of the basic tasks of their position, and both parties set goals for the next six months of things to work on. We review their pay and adjust basic duties so they can feel like they've met and discussed their performance and what they want from us. It's a mutual meeting to discuss both sides, and it's a chance for everyone to decide how we all get better. They are our lifeblood, our partners, and we need them to succeed and be successful.

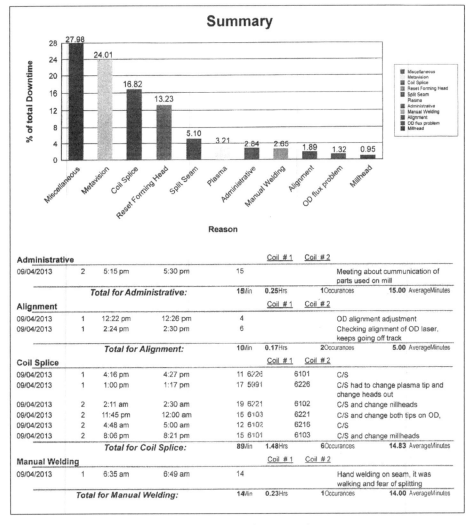

Early tracking system used to report downtime

A little discovery I have made is that stars like to have their names in lights. People appreciate when they are recognized for their efforts. By posting the numbers of each shop worker, we know whom to reward and whom to help.

When you pick a critical number, or benchmark, it has a way of dissolving employee misconceptions. Most people tend to think they accomplish more than they do. But having the critical number along with the numbers of each employee nips this in the bud. The numbers do not lie, and each team member can instantly tell if they are winning or losing the game.

Put Someone in Charge of Every Category

It's critical each department knows their starting point and how to project the future. Nick Saban often says, "I can take good news and bad news, but not surprises." Having a budget ensures there are no surprises, and everyone remains on the same page.

Trinity has a sales budget and an expense budget that guides every step and move we make. This sounds so basic, but without a budget, how can you know where you are going or where you have been? It all comes back to that phrase I love to repeat: *If it's worth doing, it's worth measuring.*

When we do open-book leadership, someone oversees every category or line item of the income statement. This is so important and invaluable to our success. At Trinity we have more than forty line items we track. The

> Having a budget ensures there are no surprises, and everyone remains on the same page.

only way this is possible is through having multiple voices on the same page. We have one person take over four line items, meaning we need ten people to cover each of these categories.

These members meet twice a month to review the numbers coming in, and they present their category in the big monthly finance meeting with the whole company.

Personally, I find this process fascinating, and it makes our monthly team meetings much more exciting. During our conversation, I call out to the people responsible for each line item, and they provide an update. There is a lot of chatter, back-and-forth conversation, and collective interaction.

Every category is covered because everyone works together.

Create Incentives That Attract Attention

Strong incentives are the key to effective motivation. Employees will not be inclined to move the needle if there is no value to them personally. You cannot rely on the fact that you are paying them to do their job. You need to motivate them if you want them to go above and beyond and feel valued. This is so important for us at Trinity, but it is even more important in today's culture. People want to feel like their efforts are appreciated. You can get away with casting vision and trying to get people to buy in for only so long.

Going back to that Jack Stack line, at some point people throw up their hands and say, "Skip the praise and give us the raise!" It's not enough to talk big and build people up. You must deliver in a way that helps *their* bottom line—like $13,541 in profit sharing incentives!

In the early days, I tried to be cute and develop fun prize incentives such as gift cards or hams, but after a few conversations I realized all most of the employees cared about was cash. We still offer incentives such as flat-screen giveaways to promote safety drives, but when I really want to motivate people to action, nothing moves the needle quite like cold hard cash. Our weeks are scheduled by the jobs we have, and incentives are paid accordingly.

If large cash incentives are not an option, you might try offering a monthly raffle for a nice dinner, sports tickets, or a TV. The key is to figure out what you can afford and create a strong enough incentive that motivates your team to action.

The key is to motivate people to produce at a certain standard, without sacrificing quality. Our rule at Trinity is that if there is a mistake in production that gets out to a client, the workers lose two weeks of incentive pay. Fortunately, this seldom happens, because our team has learned to do it right and not cut corners.

Creating a strong incentive program doesn't happen overnight. It often takes years for it to connect with people. But as this happens and they start to consistently hit their bonuses, they, along with their spouses, begin to look at these as part of their paycheck. If they receive their check and find themselves short $300, they know what they need to do to get back on track.

Eliminate Obstacles

Thinking back to that story I shared at the beginning of chapter 1, I hated it when my former boss cheated me out of my commission earnings. While there was nothing I could do to fight him from a legal perspective, his tightfisted form of leadership left a sour taste in my mouth and moved me along to start my own company.

Since that point, I have resolved to always treat my employees differently. I *want* them to hit their bonuses, and I do all in my power to see them succeed. When they succeed, we all win. This means I must eliminate any obstacles that might prevent them from hitting the goals we have established.

Usually, this comes down to the basics—equipment, processes, or people. If a piece of machinery is out of commission, I make sure it is fixed. Other times I work to create stronger processes. For example, we have this enormous $450,000 crane that our teams need at different points to transfer their materials. If a worker tells me they had to wait forty-five minutes for a crane, that's a problem because we try to keep all wait times under 10 percent in our company. So while I can't go out and purchase another crane, I can make sure the process is better so that it is available to use when they need it.

And then there are those times when *people* are the challenge. It might be a slow worker or poor leader who is not managing their teams effectively. This situation would be something we'd add to our incentive list to fix. As we fix parts of our business, we take other areas and add them to the incentive plan.

Wait time would be one of these. A portion of the month's pool would be allotted to wait time, and our goal would be to drive wait times down from 10 percent to 7.5 percent. This could result in a huge production gain in our shop and doesn't require more investment—just better planning and better communication. The dollars in the incentive pool move around year to year to fix the problems we have. As soon as we solve one, there is always another challenge on the horizon.

From my viewpoint, it is my job as the leader to do several things. First, I need to listen. What are my teams saying? Then, I need to do all in my power to eliminate any excuses. Doing so holds everybody accountable and helps the process move along. It also allows me to ask questions like, "I have asked what's not working and you haven't mentioned this. Why?"

This allows me to put the "burden" on my team to come forward and tell me what's not working, and it also allows me to say, "I'm going to eliminate every obstacle in your way, but I need X in return." We share the accountability and share in the reward.

A brief example: from 2012 to 2018, when China was dumping cheap steel into the US, our company operated on a shoestring budget, and we couldn't meet our critical number of 3.5 percent to share the profits. This period was so embarrassing. Month after month I stood up and spoke about our tighter margins. I felt torn up inside. It's hard to feel like a success if you're not hitting your number. But no one in our company begrudged me, because they could read the news and see our industry was up against the ropes. Instead, they buckled down, and we worked to improve our processes and make sure we sent better-quality products out the door. Our margins for error were thin, and we couldn't afford to make a mistake or lose a customer.

During this extended season, I made sure to keep clear communication with my team. We didn't lower salaries and still paid production incentives. Another thing I did was go to Washington and do my part to lobby for the steel industry in the US.

Sometimes it felt like we were fighting an uphill battle, and I felt like I was letting our team down. Still, I wanted all of us to succeed. I wanted to get back to that 3.5-minimum mark and 5 percent critical number because it was important to me we all shared the profits.

> Every leader of a company should want to eliminate any obstacle that prevents their team from experiencing success.

From my perspective, this should be the goal of every business owner. Every leader of a company should want to eliminate any obstacle that prevents their team from experiencing success.

Evaluate Your Progress

The only way we get better is through continuously making a series of adjustments. It's looking at things like equipment, processes, and people and focusing on ways to improve.

As we have done this, our numbers have continued to improve. The key for us was we had to collect the data. As we processed the information and feedback from our teams, we knew what we needed to change to stay on track.

Back in 2015, when Trinity was at $68 million in sales, our accounting firm sat in on our January monthly finance meeting. There I shared a vision for growth and made the ambitious statement to our team that in the next three years we would hit $100 million in annual sales.

One of the accounting managers who attended that meeting was a guy named Scott, who eventually became a partner at the firm. In 2019, we hit $100 million. When we did, Scott walked into my office at Christmas and handed me a bag of a hundred of those $1 million chocolate bars.

"What's this?" I said.

"I've got a story to tell you," Scott replied. "Back in 2015, when you threw out that number of $100 million, I thought you were crazy. I thought Trinity had too many issues and areas that needed improvement. But you were right, and I was wrong!"

"Well, you just didn't know what I knew at the time!" I replied.

We had a good laugh and agreed our next stop was $250 million. As I write this, that number looks closer to $500 million, and before we know it, I know we'll be shooting for $1 billion in annual sales!

I mention this story not to brag but to point out the power of progress and of belief in what you're doing. When you have clear-cut goals and know where you want to go, anything is possible.

This is why it is important to think and dream big. If you want to swing for the fences, not only do you have to have BHAGs (big, hairy, audacious goals), but you need to have BHARs—big, hairy, audacious rewards!

I often tell my managers that they don't have to focus on everything, but they do need to focus on what is not working. Accurate numbers always tell the real story of what is and isn't working and will point you in the right direction. They are the manager, and they form the basis for every benchmark.

Takeaways

➡ If it's worth doing, it's worth measuring!

➡ If you haven't been rewarding people for their hard work, why not? Start now!

➡ Check online and with your bank if you aren't sure of the industry benchmarking standards for your business.

➡ How would you know that your team was going to miss a budget or sales number or customer delivery? Would you be able to give them a heads-up because you had the information in advance? If not, would you want to?

➡ Are your employees working for one common goal or objective?
   ◻ Think of ways to create incentives for your employees to accomplish these goals and objectives!

➡ It's important that your budget and critical numbers are visible on a scoreboard so everyone can see and understand.

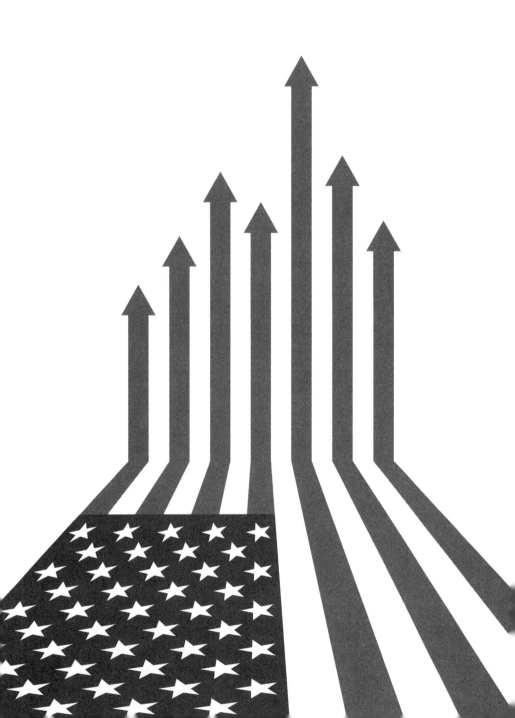

CHAPTER 6

SCOREBOARDS HELP YOU ESCAPE THE LION

We've all seen those videos of lions chasing gazelles on National Geographic.

Sometimes you see them escape, but it's always the weakest that get culled from the herd. Then they are caught, and it is all over in a matter of minutes.

Business is much like this illustration. Every CEO is a gazelle doing their best to keep ahead of the lions out to devour them. They are running, doing their best to keep from being swallowed up by larger companies who seek to snuff them out.

I never forget this illustration. Anytime I start to get complacent and take for granted things like budgeting and critical numbers, I realize that

> Every CEO is a gazelle doing their best to keep ahead of the lions out to devour them.

some business somewhere is hot on my tail. If I do not stay at the top of my game, everything can be over in a relatively short period of time.

As I mentioned earlier, I would have never imagined a company like Valley Steel, a company that had been around for decades, would go out of business seemingly overnight. One moment they were the titans of the industry, and the next they were brought to their knees. This taught me that if it could happen to them, it could happen to anyone.

I say this not to create unnecessary fear but to inject a healthy sense of motivation. Yes, business is a game, but it is a game with competitors who seek to take you out. The only way you stay ahead is to keep your eyes on what matters most—the scoreboard.

The Scoreboard Is King

After you pick your benchmark, this is the critical number that goes on your scoreboard. It is the standard by which you compare your actual production.

The scoreboard is the boss. It is the oxygen of Trinity, and it is incorporated into every level of our business. Every department creates a critical number and scoreboard so that everyone on the team knows what the goal is.

I'll give you an example. Every week Trinity makes about twenty-five coil splices. A coil splice is when you join two strips of coils end to end and weld them together to make a piece of pipe. It's part of the manufacturing process and happens every day.

As we met with others in our industry, we discovered the average benchmark for a coil splice was forty-five minutes. Through hard work and focus, we were able to get this number down to fifteen minutes—a standard rarely matched in our industry.

But about a year ago our splice times began to creep up to twenty minutes. At first it wasn't a big deal, but when this became a consistent pattern, I grew concerned. Fifteen minutes had been our standard for close to eight years. Going through my normal checklist, I knew it had to be people, equipment, or process that was holding us back. I came to find out it was a little bit of everything.

While some of our guys thought the fifteen-minute standard might be too high and asked if we should change our standard, I knew this wasn't the answer. Instead, we reviewed all our processes, fixed any equipment challenges, and spent extra time training some new folks on both shifts. Before long we were under fifteen minutes again.

This proved to be a key lesson. It reminded me that a leader must know what is right and stick to their guns. Because we had fifteen minutes so ingrained into our culture, this kept us from slipping into a new, less-productive rut.

The key to this switch was making sure our team understood what we were trying to accomplish. The faster they worked, the more money we *all* made. This wasn't me beating them up for not working hard enough. It was me coming alongside them to boost production so everyone won. Also, it gave us a chance to review our processes and confirm we just needed to eliminate obstacles and go back to the basics.

One of the ways we boosted production was through eliminating wasted time. I realized our handling process after a coil splice was less than ideal. Every time we made a cut, a worker would stick the excess steel in our backyard. The only problem was it was never in the right spot. On average, this excess steel would be shuffled around the yard two or three times before it was finally placed in its proper spot. After making this discovery, I instructed our team to eliminate these extra steps, saving us countless work hours in the process.

When the scoreboard is king, everything changes. You start to question why you do what you do and find the correct answers.

A Scoreboard Others Can't Believe

When everyone buys in and the scoreboard becomes the manager, you create standards others cannot believe.

Back in 2015, I was in Turkey with two other mill leaders taking a tour of several steel pipe plants. We were there because we wanted to see how we compared to others in our industry. There are always ways to improve technology and techniques, and even simple things like shaving a minute or two off certain processes can really boost profits.

Because the company that sold us our pipe mill was from Turkey, they wanted to give us the grand tour of their headquarters and one of the new pipe mills they had installed. As the plant manager showed us around, he asked how long it took our team to complete a coil splice. When I responded with fifteen minutes, he couldn't believe it and told me as much. A coil splice in that amount of time seemed unfathomable to him, and the only plausible explanation was that we weren't telling the truth.

When I returned home the next week, I looked up our coil splice time for the week and saw we had indeed averaged under fifteen minutes. I sent the report to the owner of the pipe mill manufacturer and asked him to pass along the numbers to the mill manager.

His response made me smile. "That's the reason I love you, Robert!" he said.

This fun interaction reminded me of the importance of setting a clear scoreboard with clear goals in mind to measure and monitor. Without it, we would have probably remained indefinitely at the thirty-minute mark we'd started at. And while this number was better than most of our competitors, by cutting this time in half to fifteen minutes, we were able to reduce hundreds of work hours—adding up to around $1.5 million a year in potential profits!

It just goes to show that the power of processes done well over extended periods of time and illustrates the difference between organizations that make a profit and those that set the standard.

Unfortunately, as I have traveled around to different companies, there is often a culture of fear that permeates the atmosphere. Employees are afraid to make a mistake because they worry it might cost them their job. Managers and those in leadership make statements like, "Because we've always done it this way," "Because I said so," or "We're too busy to change." These are all signs they are headed in the wrong direction.

If you find yourself making these types of statements, stop. Take intentional steps to change your language, be more inclusive, and build a culture of trust. If you are a manager with the sole focus of keeping your job, pause and evaluate your motives. Ask yourself how you are growing your team. Have you settled into a role where you have stopped caring about the development of those below you on the org chart?

And if you are working at a company that makes you live in fear for your job and creates an atmosphere of distrust, move on. Find an organization that has the proper values and is headed in a better direction.

Hey, if you can't find one, pick up your phone and call Trinity Products at 1-800-456-7473 and ask to speak to Robert Griggs! If you are the type of person who is ambitious and has high standards, you're just the individual we want on our team.

PIPE DIVISION

Sale Rep	Yesterday Orders	Weekly Orders	MTD Orders	MTD Mill Tons	MTD Profit	YTD Orders	Revenue Goal	YTD Mill Tons	YTD Profit	Profit Goal	YTD Profit %	YTD Billing
AJ Griggs	0	0	0	0	0	21,125,339	14,075,000	9,912	7,845,964	2,910,500	37%	16,359,958
Justin Herren	6,582,984	6,650,304	6,650,304	4,280	2,636,242	14,302,121	11,575,000	4,711	4,798,777	2,321,500	34%	8,112,254
Adam Manz	26,704	116,820	116,820	54	41,129	13,057,170	4,000,000	4,756	4,743,073	883,500	36%	10,336,549
Tony Baker	0	60,650	119,950	50	32,851	9,171,682	6,525,000	2,804	3,763,336	2,620,500	41%	8,335,232
Jeff Nuernberger	0	0	17,650	10	3,900	11,202,613	8,950,000	3,020	3,469,233	1,863,500	31%	10,462,413
Tim Ransom	115,450	180,700	212,185	113	80,152	7,031,249	5,300,000	2,785	2,602,081	1,611,000	37%	3,640,812
Pete Carnaghi	0	50,361	79,599	41	25,991	7,272,401	8,475,000	3,094	2,427,433	1,905,500	33%	6,484,604
Garrett James	2,980	2,980	2,980	0	880	5,060,589	6,250,000	1,626	1,930,625	2,176,500	38%	5,231,166
Luke Crump	0	0	0	0	0	6,651,565	11,270,000	2,244	1,890,273	2,134,700	28%	14,565,104
Kyle Richardson	0	270,100	275,000	48	110,328	5,666,158	6,050,000	482	1,638,422	2,232,000	29%	6,282,009
Matt Austin	4,117	4,960	4,960	2	1,652	3,075,108	3,085,000	1,260	1,064,479	656,550	35%	3,757,564
Buddy Sumpter	0	0	0	0	0	2,324,063	3,500,000	1,115	789,945	740,000	34%	2,407,705
Clayton Stark	0	0	0	0	0	3,001,954	0	507	627,481	0	21%	1,723,851
Jeff Ware	0	0	0	0	0	401,091	5,425,000	190	221,782	1,157,650	55%	515,597
Mike Laukaitis	0	0	0	0	0	318,521	0	50	69,201	0	22%	964,891
Rich Revolinsky	0	0	0	0	0	237,798	4,120,000	35	59,802	1,408,500	25%	767,147
Jonathan Sprague	0	0	0	0	0	0	0	0	0	0	0%	0
Total:	$6,732,235	$7,336,875	$7,479,448	4,596	2,933,126	$109,899,423	$98,600,000	38,590	$37,941,907	$24,621,900	35%	$99,946,856

The Beauty of the Scoreboard

A well-done scoreboard is a beautiful thing, and I have made it a point to track everything we think important. Here is an example.

I've mentioned that we build a weekly production schedule based on our time on task number, coil splice time, and size change over time. We build the schedule and then budget accordingly. Then we track it shift by shift, day after day. If we are off schedule, we ask why and try to figure out how we can get back on track. As we repeat this process, we gather more data, build a stronger model, and live up to a higher set of standards. Because we track, we almost never miss our tonnage production pipe goals two weeks in a row.

A couple of years ago we hired a new director of operations who came from outside our circle and struggled at first to get our culture and embrace our expectations. He could not believe how open and inclusive we were. Initially I was excited to have him on board because he came with a strong résumé and great scheduling skills, and he had been involved in an aerospace organization that was way larger than ours and more sophisticated. It seemed like a match made in heaven.

But around a year into this marriage, I noticed we missed our tonnage goal three weeks in a row. Because this almost never happened, I got more involved in the process, and I refocused our team on the basics and the scoreboard. For a few weeks, things changed, and we began to hit our goals again. But then, after the pressure lifted, we went right back to missing six out of the next ten weeks. I knew something was up.

If I had been fuzzy on the numbers, it's possible this new director might have remained on the team longer. But because I valued the scoreboard, I knew when things went off the rails. Coming back to that all-important question, I asked myself, "Is it people, processes, or equipment?" A short review told me it was the new manager who was the problem. Despite his credentials, he had not bought into our system and was now standing in the way of our team's growth. A few months later, I let him go, and he moved on to another company.

Since then, we have promoted from within and gotten right back to meeting our weekly tonnage goals. We have standards at our organization, and when these standards are not met, we must know why. Many times it's a simple fix. It might be a personnel (this has been the case a lot lately with the current labor market) or equipment issue. But when we understand what the problem is, everyone on the team rallies to create a solution. When someone on our team asks for help, we call this "throwing the flag," and I view it as a sign of strength, not weakness. While it takes a while for folks to believe this, it is a sign of strength.

Throwing the flag means you have a problem, and you can use some help. We all get to places where we are confused or are too close to the problem to see a solution. When this happens, everyone on the team jumps in to help. It's a beautiful thing.

I witnessed a perfect example of this in a recent sales meeting. One of the ongoing challenges we face at the mill is that our best workers are getting poached by companies who offer something we cannot. It might be a job closer to home or overpaying workers at a rate we cannot afford. This results in labor shortages and the need to train new workers. In the past few weeks, we lost three equipment operators. As a result, this means a job that took two to three days to complete now requires three to five.

Because our mill workers have solid communication with our sales team, they gave them the heads-up. This helps on so many levels. For starters, it helps salespeople provide accurate estimates to prospective clients and set the correct expectations. Rather than constantly overpromising and underdelivering, they are setting the correct expectations.

Without the scoreboard, the incentive to collaborate with others is gone. But with it, everyone is on the same page because they all share in the profits. When you think about it, this is the dream scenario so many CEOs only wish they had: a system that alerts you when there are problems and allows people to step in and make the necessary adjustments.

This is the beauty of the scoreboard.

The Griggs Law

I have a law that goes like this: *The universe only gives you opportunities when you are least prepared to take them.* Every time I've wanted to do something big, it's felt like the timing was off. I don't have enough capital on hand, or I feel comfortable and don't want to take another risk. But when I know the right thing to do, I do it.

Here is a key example. At Trinity, we ship over 2,500 truckloads of steel a year to locations across the US. Ten years ago, while we had our own trucks, we could not ship other companies' freight on our trucks. Because the federal government controls how the trucking industry runs, they give you permission when you meet certain qualifications to haul for others. It's called an authority.

> The universe only gives you opportunities when you are least prepared to take them.

Knowing there was some potential in this industry, I suggested we separate the freight department into a stand-alone company that could broker loads of freight for other customers. After several months of discussion, the management team was still lukewarm on the idea. They felt it was going to be more work than it was worth.

Personally, I loved the idea. But seeing their hesitancy, I decided to create a separate business that was not tied to Trinity and run it as a Griggs family operation. It would be owned by my wife, Shelly, and our two sons, AJ and Bo.

Trinity closed out its traffic department, and we worked out an arrangement with one of my sons to run the new freight company. Because Bo had started in the traffic department when he first came on board at Trinity, he knew what he was doing, and it proved to be a seamless transition. Together, all three of them created National Flatbed Solutions (NFS) and purchased all Trinity's equipment at book value and handled all our freight costs for a 6 percent markup.

When we did this, several things happened. First, Trinity lost $200,000 plus in overhead. All our maintenance costs on this equipment were eliminated, and we received the money for the sale of the equipment. In addition, we made a fascinating discovery. Because the new company was discounting their payments to the other carriers, they received lower rates. And because NFS was no longer a part of Trinity, and forced a set of standard rates for shipments, we found out we came out further ahead on our margins. In the past, if a salesperson feared they would lose a sale, they would lower the shipping costs or not mark up the freight at all because it was part of the "in-house package." Now that was no longer an option.

Prior to this point, our freight margins were between 6 and 8 percent. Since we made this transition, our margins jumped to 12 to 15 percent on top of the 6 percent the new company charged. In the past, Trinity should have been making somewhere between an 18 and 21 percent margin on all our freight over the years we had been doing it in house. With $10 million in freight, we should have made $1.8

million in profit. But because our system was flawed, we made under $600,000 or barely broke even when head count and maintenance costs were factored in.

In return, NFS started off with a steady client, providing a firm foundation. It is now a successful business, buying more trucks and turning a nice profit. Their revenue for 2021 was $20 million, and they continue to grow. This is the value of staying open to opportunities.

NFS has a big, hairy, audacious goal of $100 million in sales, and I am confident it is only a matter of time until they hit it.

How a Scoreboard Can Save You $756,000

Ever since we started this new form of open-book leadership, created benchmarks, and kept our eye on the scoreboard, everything has changed. There are dozens of stories I could tell, but here are just a few.

The first deals with our monthly review of weekly mill maintenance and production numbers—our scoreboard time. This is the place where we review the week's rolling schedule, downtime, and consumables (such as wire, flux, and other components needed to make pipe), and it is where we get a feel for how each operation is running.

At these meetings, we invite a team of people who are directly working on the mill. These include maintenance, mill operators, payout welders, and plasma operators. Everyone gets a chance to sit in on these sessions, and occasionally we are joined by guests who supply product to the mill. This allows them to see the process and understand the items we're following.

About two years into the process, the topic of scrap came up at one of our meetings. I mentioned that we had about 8 percent scrap on all the tons going through the mill. A young man in the back casually piped up and said, "Well, I could cut the starter pipe scrap in half by turning the welders on earlier."

The meeting continued, but after a minute my mind suddenly clued in to what he had said. "Wait a second," I told him. "You're telling me we could cut our scrap in half if we just turned the welders on sooner?" He nodded and went on to explain. When the welders produced a new size of pipe, they had to form the coil to the proper diameter. This is a process called threading the mill, and this always used up about forty feet of pipe just to get the process started. But by turning the welders on at only ten to twelve feet, we could cut our waste pile in half.

When I asked him why on earth we'd always done forty feet of pipe in the past, he shrugged and said, "That's the way we were trained by the guys who installed the mill." As you might be able to tell, I hate answers that start with, "Because that's the way we've always done it!"

That statement he made gave me flashbacks to the lion-and-gazelle illustration. With this type of thinking, I knew we were behaving like a gazelle that wanted to be caught. I stopped the meeting and pulled out a spreadsheet.

Doing some quick calculations, I realized we were scrapping sixty-three tons of pipe a month. If we turned the welders on early, we could conservatively cut this in half. Because pipe sold for $1,000 a ton, this meant we were looking at $63,000 in savings every month, or $756,000 a year.

Since we made this discovery, I cannot tell you how many mills I have toured and found the starter pipe is forty feet or longer. Every day they discard thousands of dollars in profit, all because no one has thought to do it better.

Looking back, I am convinced the scoreboard is the reason we made it through the down years of 2012 to 2018. Because we were able to track our time, energy, and resources, we knew how to operate on a tight budget when times were tough. And now that times are better, we are that much more ahead of the game.

This is why a scoreboard and regular discussion meetings with everyone on your team is so important. Without them, you end up doing business as it has always been done, with little reason behind your actions. But when you know the numbers and what it takes to win, you will be much more motivated to eliminate any areas of waste and create more savings.

Always Keep Score

At our monthly maintenance meeting, we always track any stoppages we have in the pipe mill to ensure our processes are working efficiently. There are dozens of things that can go wrong, such as mechanical breakdowns or operational issues. When our pipe mill machine stops, I want to know why.

About three years into producing pipe, someone suggested in our meeting that we should begin checking these problems by total time and frequency. Through this new strategy, we noticed an interesting pattern. The number one cause of downtime was a certain loose bracket that held one of our lasers in place.

A short investigation revealed it was coming loose more than twice a day. Each time, this would cost around two to three minutes of downtime, totaling to around twenty hours of stoppage time a year. Because our pipe mill produced around $3,000 an hour, this meant we sacrificed a profit of around $60,000—all because of a busted bracket. This shocked me. Why was it that no one had done anything about it?

The solution cost us less than $500 and took only a few minutes to fix. Without a scoreboarding system that tracked the frequency of downtime, it's likely this trend would have continued for several more months, costing us thousands in the process. But because we had a scoreboard, we were able to provide a quick fix.

> **It's tough to win the game if you never keep track of the score.**

Remember, it's tough to win the game if you never keep track of the score.

Do It Right!

I'm an avid St. Louis Blues hockey fan. And if you ever go to a professional hockey game, you'll notice that when the linesmen go to drop the puck to start play, they often have opposing players reset and reestablish their position. One or both centers will be asked to leave the drop zone, and another player or players will come in to take the draw. Officially, the rules say that two violations result in a penalty. But there is a funny thing that happens. While the centers who take the face-off might get kicked out of the draw because of some infringement, the second center who comes in almost never gets called. The linesmen scrutinize and kick players out the first time but drop the puck instantly the second time.

While some of this could be chalked up to greater caution exhibited by the new face-off player, you can't tell me there isn't a better way to get it right the first time.

This principle applies to business. The other day I was sitting in one of our meetings and listening to one of the ways our teams had misfired on their first attempt at a project but came back and got it right the second time. This left me to exclaim, "Why can't we get it right the first time?"

Unfortunately, for many people, there is a mindset that tempts them to take it easy on their first attempt and get it right the second go-around. I think this is terrible, counterproductive, and drags everyone down in the end. While there is something to be said about learning from past mistakes, there is also something that needs to be said about showing up and doing the right thing the right way the first time. This is what a professional does.

While the last three chapters might have felt like a bit of a whirlwind, they come as one package. Everything ties together. When you commit to open-book leadership, this takes shape only as you pick that critical number and benchmark. After you do this, these numbers become your scoreboard. It's that simple.

If you are new to this process, here is a short recap that can serve as your game plan and attempt to do business the right way.

STEP 1: ASK YOURSELF THE TOUGH QUESTIONS

Are you a leader? Do you struggle in this area? Are you willing to grow? Will you engage in tough conversations, even if you feel stretched and uncomfortable in the process?

It's OK if you need to develop your leadership skills. We all do. But the key is your willingness to change and improve. If you want others to be open and transparent, you must model this by example.

STEP 2: BE HONEST ABOUT WHERE YOU ARE

If you have some of the systems and structures I mentioned already in play at your company, that's great. You're in the top percentile. Take what you learn here and use it as a stepping-stone to further your development.

However, if your organization is a mess and there is a strong culture of distrust, be realistic. Start small and work to implement change. Do the little things with excellence. Keep a detailed budget. Get to know the personalities on your team and begin to instill in them the basics of open-book leadership.

STEP 3: PICK A NUMBER THAT IS REALISTIC

After your team gets on board, begin the benchmarking process by picking your critical number. If you are a manager, but not a business owner, have the conversation with your CEO and ask them if this new form of operation is a possibility. Work with your team to create a clear number that is a win for the organization. If you work for someone who knows what they are doing, this should be a no-brainer.

Don't shoot for the moon. Start with baby steps and allow your team to get some wins under their belt. Pick numbers you can hit.

STEP 4: OFFER A COMPELLING INCENTIVE

Remember, if your employees do not care about the incentive, they will not care to meet your goal.

Again, if you're a manager, work with your boss to offer incentives that will attract attention. A great place to start is with a free lunch. Cook a BBQ for your team and demonstrate that you are all in. There are many ways you can incentivize people, but remember that basic universal truth—humans are motivated by the green stuff!

STEP 5: HELP PEOPLE WIN

Next, make it your goal to see your team win. Like a general leading their team into battle, it is your responsibility to set the pace.

Nothing will create buy-in quite like helping people achieve a series of personal victories. If you notice someone struggling to pull their way, coach them. Build them up so they can share in the profits. Reward the ones who are doing it well.

Do not make it a habit to change the goal line in the middle of the game, but do your best to help people win.

STEP 6: EVALUATE YOUR PROGRESS AND ADJUST

Remember, when we first started this open-book leadership, benchmarking, and scoreboarding business, everyone was nervous. We made mistakes by picking wrong numbers, hiring the wrong people, and offering wrong incentives. This is par for the course.

Eventually, we calmed down. Now we can hit our numbers with good accuracy, and when we miss them, we readjust and refocus.

STEP 7: HAVE FUN!

I cannot stress this enough. Business is a serious game with real-world implications, but it can be so enjoyable. It doesn't have to be a continual drag. As I keep saying, if you do the hard work and create strong systems, you can reap the rewards down the road.

At this point in our company's history, I look forward to going to work. While many in my industry cannot wait for retirement, I enjoy walking into the office and saying, "I love the pipe business!" (to which everyone laughs). Yes, we still have challenges that sometimes keep me up at night, but the joy of building a great organization with a tremendous team of people energizes me.

It makes me want to keep going when times are tough. To me, life and business are just the grown-ups' version of Monopoly. You work hard to win, but at the end of the day, all the pieces go back in the box. What you have left are the memories and relationships you have built along the way.

Numbers give you power. They keep you from accepting excuses and offer a road map to continuously improve.

Takeaways

➡ Do it right the first time, every time! You don't want to spend the money and energy having to try a second time.

➡ Have you ever thought about what might put your company out of business or hurt it badly? You should brainstorm with your team about this and make a list of things to avoid.

➡ How can scoreboards help you in your daily business? List daily or weekly scoreboards and think about what you want to be warned about in advance.

➡ Have you ever been talked into lowering your standards? For what reason, and do you think it helped?

➡ What are some ways you find yourself doing the job two or three times instead of just once? Can you list those times? By doing the job multiple times instead of getting it right the first time, you are wasting money and energy.

➡ Do you have employees who pass work down to others despite it being their task? You must engage those employees and have them be open and honest with you.

➡ Do your employees trust you? They shouldn't be afraid to make a mistake and should be able to tell you about any of their questions and concerns. You should also encourage discussion on what things may or may not be working within the company.

➡ Have your managers ever said any of the following?

    □ "We've always done it that way!"

    □ "We're too busy to change or try new approaches."

    □ "We're fine as is."

➡ If any of the above is true, immediately put a stop to that attitude and move forward without them.

➡ Hold meetings where people see how you lead and manage—if you have done this before, list some ways you think it might've helped among your employees.

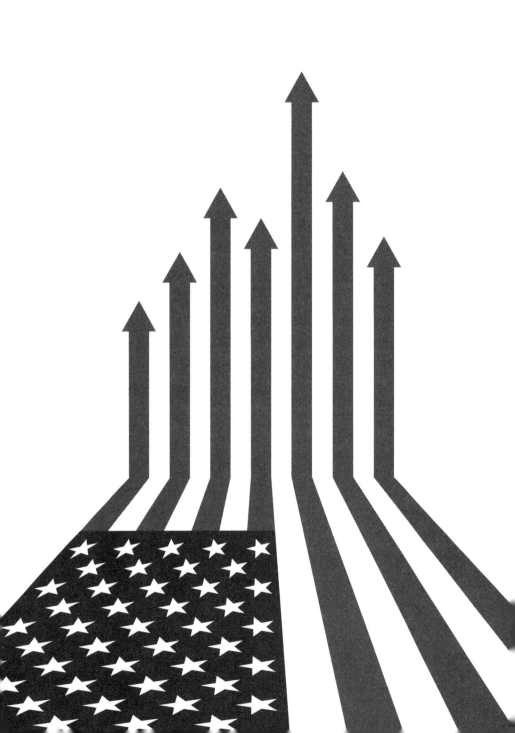

CHAPTER 7

CONTINUOUS IMPROVEMENT

Following the Second World War, the Japanese economy was in shambles. Beyond the obvious devastation of Hiroshima and Nagasaki, other cities like Tokyo were shadows of their former glory. Firebombing missions like Operation Meetinghouse leveled sixteen square miles of the capital city, devastating Japan's economy in the process.

With the conclusion of the war, something needed to be done to revitalize a nation that was in decline. By this point, Japan's manufacturing processes were so poor that many of their products could not compare with foreign competitors. They largely exported low-quality products with flawed designs.

But in the next thirty years, all of this changed, and Japan became one of the leading manufacturers in the world. Instead of Japanese officials making trips to the United States to learn best practices of production, the roles reversed, and the United States' business leaders started going to Japan to learn why their economy had been completely transformed in only a few decades. As they would discover, the key to this change was the institution of a new strategy—continuous improvement.

The leader of this movement in Japan was W. Edwards Deming. Always an outside-the-box thinker, Deming's grander ideas never took root in the United States. But in 1950, Deming traveled to Japan and met with hundreds of industrial leaders.

Per his bio, Deming "taught top managers and engineers the methods for improving how they worked and learned together. His focus was both internally, between departments, and externally, with their suppliers and customers."[14]

"I was the only man in 1950 that believed that the Japanese could invade the markets of the world and would within four years,"[15] he told one reporter. Deming's system of quality production through statistical analysis was just the boost this fledgling economy needed. "What I saw was a magnificent workforce, unsurpassed management, and the best statistical ability in the world. It seemed to me that those three forces could be put together, and I put them together so that Japanese quality, instead of being shoddy, became known within a few years—in less than four years, manufacturers all over the world were screaming for protection."[16]

The key for Japan was urgency. They were ready to work hard and try because each worker wanted to provide a better lifestyle for their

---

14 "Deming the Man," The Deming Institute, accessed January 19, 2022, https://deming.org/deming-the-man/.

15 "If Japan Can, Why Can't We?" Deming Institute YouTube Channel, November 19, 2015, https://www.youtube.com/watch?v=vcG_Pmt_Ny4&ab_channel=DemingInstitute.

16 Ibid.

family. There was a Japanese mindset that said they were not in it just for individual success but for the success of the group.

From Deming's perspective, the beauty of continuous improvement was that there were no additional costs. You were not hiring new workers or purchasing an expensive piece of equipment. Instead, you took what you had and made it better. For industrial plants, this meant evaluating each step of the production line and observing which areas needed to be changed to produce at a higher level.

Through using statistical analysis, Deming eliminated the guessing game. From his perspective, the key was to have the people who were doing the work monitor the system and make suggestions for improvement. Contrary to business owners who tended to blame workers for poor production, according to Deming, 85 percent of the problem was management.[17]

Personally, I look at Deming's challenge here and see it as an issue of leadership. What he saw were a bunch of managers—people who viewed their teams as cogs in a wheel. Instead, what he really needed was leaders.

Deming was often referred to as the third wave of the Industrial Revolution. There were the first two waves with inventions such as the cotton gin followed by mass manufacturing. But lacking in these two revolutions was a statistical structure of quality control.

In the 1980s, various companies in the US, such as Ford, Toyota, Xerox, Ricoh, Sony, and Procter & Gamble, experienced revitalization after adopting Deming's system of continuous improvement.[18]

---

17   Ibid.

18   "Deming the Man," The Deming Institute, accessed January 19, 2022, https://deming.org/deming-the-man/.

The Value of Continuous Improvement

In an odd way, when large corporations started to embrace this mindset, continuous improvement took on a big business image. Many smaller companies thought of it as a complex system that only the big guys could do. But as I will argue in this chapter, it doesn't need to be this way. Continuous improvement is a process any company, at any level, can implement.

Continuous improvement has transformed our culture at Trinity. When we first started our journey into open-book leadership back in 2000, the financial literacy part was one of the first steps we took with our teams. But as time went on, I felt like the continuous improvement component was a needed addition. It was a way to teach our teams they could change the bottom-line numbers through their feedback and ideas.

At the time, we were doing $6.7 million in annual sales. Fast-forward a decade, and by 2010 we were at $54 million. By 2018 we were at $103 million, and at the close of 2021 we finished out the year at over $200 million. That same continuous improvement propelled our sales to our greatest heights with over $300 million in 2022, and projected budget growth in 2026 for over $600 million. While some of this growth can be attributed to the price of steel, much comes down to our commitment to continuous improvement. None of this new growth has come through acquisition, which is a testament to what the Trinity team has accomplished.

The larger you grow, the more your structures and systems are exposed.

Thanks to continuous improvement, our rate of growth continues to accelerate, and we end up doubling our company in fewer and fewer years. Without it, there is no possible way we would be at the level we are today. There would be too many holes in our boat.

As I have discovered, the larger you grow, the more your structures and systems are exposed. If you have a flawed setup at the start, expect those flaws to magnify as you experience more pressure. Through continuous improvement, we now have processes and procedures in place so we can hit larger targets in faster times.

What I love about continuous improvement is that it is the mechanism by which you fix and improve your entire system. It's methodical, simple, and repeatable.

Learning the Cycle of Success

Back in 2011, I was introduced to the Cycle of Success Institute (COSI). Every month, a representative from this organization taught our leadership team the basic building blocks of continuous improvement.

We had conversations about our org chart, conducted employee surveys, created better organizational habits, outlined our priorities, solved problems, and established committees to take care of challenges.

The whole goal of COSI is a four-step process that revolves around the following points.

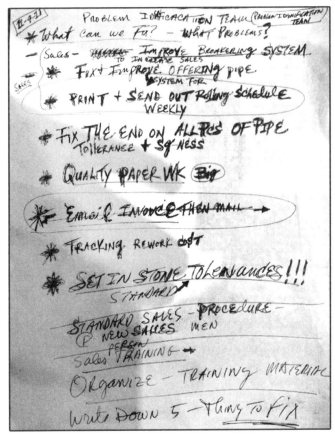

Original meeting list from our first COSI meeting PIT team on November 9, 2011

POINT 1: DISCOVERING

This involves gathering information, learning from your employees, and remembering their ideas are incredibly valuable. At this stage, it's all about garnering feedback and collecting as many diverse opinions as possible. You want to expand your net and hear what those low and high on the org chart are saying.

POINT 2: IMPLEMENTING

This step empowers your people to get involved in teams that implement the best ideas. You're saying, "OK, who is the best person to tackle this problem?" Or you're asking, "What people do we need to work together to finish this task?" Collaboration should be high as you work to implement solutions.

POINT 3: ALIGNING

This is about better aligning your company with communication, accountability, and success. You're not just getting on the same page to complete a single project. Instead, you're figuring out how every department can have the same mindset with everything they do.

POINT 4: SUSTAINING

This last step is about building a winning workplace culture that builds long-term, sustainable growth. This is something I have thought a lot about as it relates to Trinity. The last thing I want to do is create a model that fizzles out in a year or two. And I believe the last few decades have demonstrated our team's commitment to sustainable growth.

And as the years have progressed, we have taken these four points and implemented our own four-step approach.

STEP 1: COLLECT FEEDBACK

We start with a group meeting by department, and it continues in our monthly finance meeting. As I referenced in the previous chapters, our goal is to find what isn't working and further develop what is. I like to ask, "What is giving you the most pain, and how can we fix it?"

In the department meeting everyone gets a sticky note, and they start scribbling down suggestions. I always beg them to be honest, and for the most part, they are. We always make sure to take our time, because as the meeting goes on, more people contribute and make suggestions. Here are a few of the questions I gave and some of the raw comments I received in one of our first office surveys.

Question 1: If you were in charge of the entire organization, what are the first three things you would try to accomplish?

- "More equipment for the guys to do their job faster and easier."

- "Pay structure for floor employees on grading scale."

- "Remove salesmen who are not bringing anything to the table and replace them with new guys who have the drive to get new business."

- "I would establish a person dedicated to cold-calling engineers."

Question 2: What three things would most improve your job?
- "An espresso machine."

- "Don't use loader sheets to schedule fab work or cutting schedule."

- "Having a department at the mill dedicated to cutting pipe AND midwelds."

- "More time given for mandatory paperwork."

Question 3: What three things do you most dislike about your job?

- "Working in office. I have dogs and kids at home. I can do my job at home with no impact on my performance."

- "Communication is not always consistent or clear."

- "There is no longer a manager that directly communicates with sales reps on a personal or professional level to provide support."

- "Constant repetitive questions about the same topic from salespeople."

This selection is just the office department alone, and these answers represent just a few of the dozens of suggestions I received in our meeting. As with any survey, some of the ideas are easier to fix than others, and some cannot be implemented at all. But the point is we listen and always look for ways to improve. We trust our employees and want to hear what they have to say.

Our goal is to write down on paper what the members of our teams are saying, decide if we can do something to help, and then place their suggestions in one of seven categories.

SUGGESTION BOX

This is an old-school idea, but we found that a suggestion box with a lock on it located in different parts of the building was invaluable!

Our COO, Jim Nazzoli, had the key and pulled the suggestions out of the box before the big Finance Meeting; I reviewed the suggestions and he sanitized them!

These suggestions allowed the team to understand that we are listening and actively working to fix problems. The team has a strong voice—the suggestion box will tell them, "If you are nervous about how your thoughts will be received, you can do it anonymously!"

This is also a great equalizer for leaders to help the team understand that 100 percent of things can't be fixed without knowing about them!

STEP 2: CATEGORIZE THE SUGGESTIONS

Every suggestion I receive will fall into one of seven categories I call the Seven Ms. By organizing these ideas, we make sure no idea falls through the cracks and ensure the right people tackle these challenges.

So, for example, let's take a few more of these raw suggestions I received and place them in their designated areas.

Manpower

- "Hire more fabricated welders/fitters, pipe cutters."

- "I would research hiring a person dedicated to managing big projects for the whole company; he would be dedicated to building stronger relationships with vendors we use and contractors we team up with."

- "Continued investment in people, new product lines, and equipment to keep us growing, which will grow the value of Trinity."

Machinery

- "New burn table and more efficient workflow setup for street plate burn/weld."

- "Espresso machine."

- "New or updated welding equipment."

Materials

- "Have pipe ready in yard."

- "More equipment for the guys to do their job faster and easier."

- "New mouse pad / office phone / tables."

Methods

- "Automate the entire order entry process so that all departments get notified when jobs come into the system that need their attention."

- "Four ten-hour days with Fridays off."

- "Ability to do continuing education."
- "Add more details to mill inventory work orders like M and M Domestic … Needs coil MTRs."

Management

- "Ensure all people are held with the same accountability."
- "Uniformity in processes for all departments."
- "Generate five-year master plan for growth and review quarterly."
- "Continued investment in people, new product lines, and equipment to keep us growing, which will grow the value of Trinity."

Money

- "Pay Down Debt."
- "Insurance that covered more, with less deductibles."
- "Once travel is allowed, increase travel for sales for better relationship building w/ customers."

Marketing

- "Continue to push Tri-Loc development."
- "I would establish a person dedicated to cold-calling engineers."
- "Increase sales support."
- "Reduce sales force (salespeople)."

As I write this, many of these suggestions have already been implemented. It's important to note there are different types of people who provide feedback. You have the ones who say, "Everything is great! I love my job." Then you have wise guys, like the one who suggested we purchase an espresso machine. Sometimes you have disgruntled employees who make emotional requests. Over time I have learned to listen to these individuals and have found that if you are able to build a compelling case for the way you do business, they will become some of your most loyal followers. Other times there are workers who are new and do not understand how their ideas might not be practical to implement, at least in the foreseeable future.

But laying these outliers aside, most of the comments I receive are very good. And the longer someone is on our team, the better their suggestions become. The key is to make sure your employees know you value their input. You're not just going through the obligatory motion of asking them what they think. Instead, you care about their opinions enough to do something about them.

This is why it is critical to file all suggestions under one of these seven categories. It ensures valuable ideas do not fall through the cracks. Then, after you have all the suggestions in these seven categories, you evaluate which ones to tackle first. Some of these projects are easy and can be tackled that same day. Others might be long-term strategic decisions or too expensive to confront in the moment.

Whenever you collect feedback, one tip I would suggest is to get some quick wins under your belt. Focus on those ideas that are easy to implement and make a big deal when you do this. Doing so lets everyone know you value their feedback. It's a bit like debt. When you pay off one credit card, even if it is just a few hundred bucks, it gives you momentum to address the next mountain.

But from a business perspective, you also want to implement suggestions that will give you the greatest return on your investment. As I have shared in previous chapters, sometimes a quick, inexpensive fix can save thousands of dollars.

The key is to take the top three manageable suggestions in each category and then develop action teams to solve the problems.

STEP 3: SOLVE THE PROBLEM

Our action teams are called problem identification teams (or PITs). PITs are assigned to each problem and given the responsibility of coming up with possible solutions, assuming there is one. Their job is to get to the root cause of a problem.

PITs usually comprise about three to five people, with a lead person who's close to the issue. If it's welding, this means we have a fabrication manager, a welder, and someone from the office and sales. We always have an office and salesperson because this is such a critical component and invaluable to others on the team. Welders see what it takes to make the paperwork happen and get billed, and salespeople learn how difficult the shop jobs are. As a result, everyone starts to have some appreciation that all jobs are important.

Without all the parts working together, you don't have a business. It's a beautiful thing to watch teams start learning how to work together and solve problems. And after a while, it starts to become a routine process that doesn't feel overwhelming. And even when it is, there's a lot of help for everyone. The longer this happens, the more it becomes a part of the culture.

PITs focus in on why we need to rework or what the real issues are. They ask the tough questions. For example, let's take one of the generic suggestions given: "More equipment for the guys to do their job faster and easier."

A PIT will look at this suggestion and peel back the onion. What is driving this idea? Have there been a series of equipment malfunctions, or are guys in the shop consistently lacking the right tools to do their jobs? Or is this problem limited to one guy? Is the fix as simple as picking up an extra welding tool, or is this a larger problem that will require a significant financial investment? Or do we just need to have more training?

I am a big believer in the Shewhart cycle, which calls business leaders to plan, do, check, and act. This is the checklist I want each member of our PITs to think about as they address the problems before them. Don't push problems to the back burner. Instead, face them head on and put the team's ideas into action. And if something goes to the bottom of the list, let everyone know why.

STEP 4: GAIN MOMENTUM

After your teams get a few wins under their belts, they start to gain momentum. People learn the system and know how it works. Rather than waiting to address their problems at each monthly meeting, teams learn to adjust on the fly.

This is the value of helping employees see how their impact to the bottom line can improve their personal paychecks. When this happens, workers no longer want to wait to address problems, because doing so will cost *them* money.

Now, whenever questions or problems emerge, I have guys speaking up with, "Hey, that is a problem one of our PITs needs to solve." For example, let's say a faulty product goes out to a customer. One of the pieces of steel they received will not fit together, and they want to know why we have dropped the ball. After taking the necessary steps to go into damage control and someone has written a nonconformance report (NCR), we throw this problem to a PIT, and they get to the root cause of what happened. Was a worker feeling rushed and pushed the product out the door before it was ready? Were there inadequate parts available, and the workers "made do" with what they had? Does one of the workers need to be better trained so this does not happen again? Also, why didn't someone throw the flag somewhere in the system?

Throwing the flag is big! This needs to be learned early and talked about all the time. Throwing the flag means something doesn't feel right, or someone is worried we won't hit what we promised. In fact, just this morning I was on a call reminding one of our plants to throw flags. I see this as a sign of strength, not weakness. A lot of brains are better than a few!

The more we do this, the better this process gets and the more momentum that is gained.

Continuous Improvement Translates Well

Through continuous improvement, Trinity has become an intelligent, organized company. I am convinced we could take these basic improvement principles I have outlined in this chapter and plug them into most other companies and experience success.

It's because of this I often say Trinity is not just a steel company—despite this being our only product. What we really are is a people company that is extremely efficient. Give me any business, or something different to sell, and anybody who has been on our team for any length of time can work with this new organization to shift the culture and make things run more smoothly. It doesn't matter what our product is. Our product is our culture.

> **Trinity is not just a steel company—despite this being our only product. What we really are is a people company that is extremely efficient.**

A few days ago, I walked into our IT department. The guy in charge has been with us for seven years and remarked, "Robert, the systems we've been building could be put on any company we touch."

For example, we are in the process of opening an office in Kansas City. Years ago, this would have been a major undertaking. But now it is relatively straightforward because we simply review our standard operating procedures, transport our current systems, and implement them with new people in a different setting. While environments might change, the principles of continuous improvement remain the same.

We have what I consider to be a tremendous problem-solving system. And by learning this process of being forthright, asking questions, being humble, and solving problems, you start to accumulate and create people who are leaders and problem solvers. The reason I know this is that every major leadership position at Trinity to date is filled by someone who started at some entry-level position and over five to fifteen years grew into a leadership role. More on this in chapter 10.

Continuous Improvement Changes Your Employees' Perspective

By continuously improving the process, your employees begin to change. They embrace the process because they enjoy the incentives that come with it. And they know there's a system in place that can fix any issue or problem they have. Plus they understand the method on how it will get handled and fixed. This builds comfort that there's a system in place that can make their job easier, better, or less painful. It's not complicated or intimidating!

For example, I frequently ask leaders on our team to write down ways they can improve. As they go through different training systems, such as COSI, they realize there are indeed ways they can get better.

Here are a few of the responses I see:

- "I'm going to be a better listener."

- "I'm going to be more resourceful."

- "I need to work on not taking things too personal."

- "I will do better at understanding the technical aspects of my job."

- "I will bring more energy to the table."

- "I'll keep the big picture in mind when I plan."

Whenever I see statements like this, I smile inside because I can tell our team is getting it. They have bought into the improvement journey. They are committed to improving themselves, and they are committed to improving our company.

Continuous improvement is a life-giving process. It brings so much joy. It is a cycle that never ends as you continue to adjust and step up your game. After a good decade of continuous improvement, I know it is more important than ever because the demands of business only seem to grow more complex. With constant supply chain issues and customers that want their products as quickly as their Amazon packages arrive, it takes focus and determination to remain on top.

But this is where I come back to the importance of culture. The goal is not for Robert Griggs to have a successful company. Rather, the goal is to create a business where everyone on the team thrives by providing customers with top-quality service. We're all on this continuous improvement journey together.

> Continuous improvement is a life-giving process. It brings so much joy. It is a cycle that never ends as you continue to adjust and step up your game.

Takeaways

➡ CI doesn't require new investments, manpower, or overhead costs.

➡ If you can see the ways CI could improve your business, list them!

➡ If CI seems daunting to your organization, list them out and tackle them one by one.

➡ Ask your employees how you can help them do their jobs better and how you could help your leaders do their jobs better.

➡ A good exercise is to write the description of a particular role and have an employee in that role write the description. Do you think they will be the same? If not, why aren't they?

➡ Understand the four steps of the Cycle of Success:
   ▫ Collect Feedback
   ▫ Categorize the Suggestions
   ▫ Solve the Problem
   ▫ Gain Momentum

➡ Think about having an anonymous suggestion box for your employees to give their feedback!

➡ Think of quick-hitter issues you could fix right now.

➡ How about large issues that you could put a PIT together to fix?

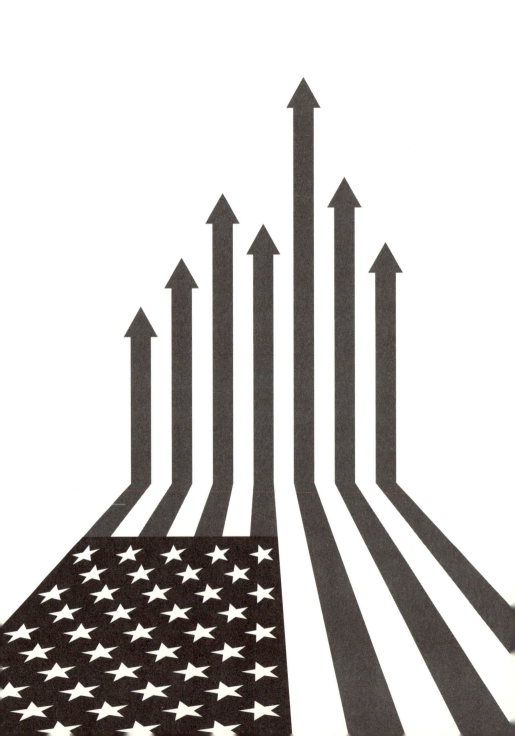

CHAPTER 8

LEADING WHEN YOU'RE NOT AT THE TOP

Up until this point, we have focused on the benefits of open-book leadership and creating a system that encourages continuous improvement.

If you are not the owner or CEO of a company, your ability to initiate change might be limited. As you read the thoughts I have laid out in this book, you might have felt a growing sense of frustration. *Yeah, Robert, I love what you're saying. But there is so little I control. Everything I do has to be run through upper levels of management, and I just don't see them having the same vision you outlined.*

Believe me, if this is where you are, I feel your pain. After all, it was my own growing frustration with poorly run companies that led me to start my own. I love the freedom that comes from being able to make my own decisions.

But even if you feel like your freedom to make decisions is limited, there is hope. There are still cost-effective baby steps you can take to shift the culture of those on your team.

The good news is that if you take these steps, you will discover all you need to know about the state of your organization. If these concepts make sense to your boss, it's a good sign you can help improve the culture. If your ideas are squelched at every turn, it is a sign you will eventually need to make a transition to another role.

A Special Thought to Managers

Whenever a midlevel manager asks me for advice on how they should lead when they are not at the top, my advice is always the same: *Start with yourself.* Lead yourself well by doing little things with excellence.

People always want to follow those they perceive are worth following—meaning they show up on time, do the right thing, own up to their mistakes, help others when needed, are humble, and go the extra mile. These are the traits of a leader, so before you think of leading others, start by being that person.

And as you do this, impart these values to your team. One of the best ways to make upper-level management notice you is by building a great team. Assuming you are in a healthy organization, the better your team is, the higher you will grow. Instead of focusing on yourself, train others to do your job. Initially, this might make you feel expendable, and there is a sense of vulnerability that sets in. But the real sign of leadership is not being afraid to see others succeed. Besides, the only way you can move up is if you make it easy for others to step in and fill your shoes when you get promoted.

Believe me, it makes it easier for your boss when you say, "I want this job, and I've trained Bill to do mine. Plus, I'll help him whenever he needs it!" This makes it easy because your boss doesn't have to worry about your old job or the new one because you're going to thrive and make him or her look like a winner.

If you are a true leader, there will always be a place for you. It might not be at the company where you are, but there will be someone out there who needs the skill set you provide. As I said earlier, nearly every management or leadership position at Trinity has been filled with someone who started in an entry-level position and was promoted up. I've always told them since the day they started to train their replacement, because I would find another higher role for them one day.

To be sure, changing your approach to leadership can be challenging, and there is the very real fear about what others might think or how we might be judged behind our backs. But if I were in your shoes, I would go about bringing change from a *project standpoint.*

Instead of going to management and telling them all about this new book you just read, make it simple. Have a conversation that goes something like this: "Listen, leading this department is a challenge, and I am always thinking about ways I can do this more effectively. With your permission, I have developed a plan to increase our productivity, solve some problems, and make everyone's job easier."

At this point, your boss will likely respond with something like, "OK, this sounds good, but what do you have in mind?"

This is when you can bring up the basic concept of continuous improvement. Show them, through a practical illustration that relates to your division of the company, how some simple action steps might create change. I'd recommend starting with a "mini game" to solve some of the company's biggest issues or pain points. Set this up as a no-lose situation. If your team does not hit these goals, it costs the company nothing. And if they do hit these new standards, the profits generated by the team more than offset any company expenses.

If at this point you are refused, this is a good indicator you are in the wrong organization. In this day and age, we have the luxury of finding jobs we can grow to enjoy. If your company isn't open to thinking differently, it might be time to look in a different direction.

But if they say yes, start with a simplified version of the whole continuous improvement process.

A Great Example of Leading in the Middle

At Trinity, I have many midlevel leaders who have the freedom to make decisions. Yes, there are still larger items they must run by their superiors, but they are granted flexibility to deal with many of the day-to-day surprises that might arise.

This morning, just before I sat down to write this section, a particular illustration stood out. I was out walking the shop floor and came across James. He is a great man with a huge beard. I love this guy, and he has been with us for fifteen years. As I walked in, he came up and gave me this huge hug and said, "I'm so lucky to be at Trinity."

A little taken aback, I asked him what he meant. He explained that right before the holiday season, his wife became very sick. She had been taken to the hospital and was placed on steroids and antibiotics. These caused an adverse reaction, forcing her to remain in the hospital for five days. Realizing he needed to be there for his family, James called his supervisor, Jim. James wasn't sure what to do because he knew he needed to stay home with the kids, but he didn't have any more personal days off. Jim's response was immediate.

"James, don't worry. We've got you covered. Take the time you need, because family comes first." Ordinarily, such requests were approved by me, but in this case, I didn't even know a thing about it—and that to me was the best part. It made me incredibly happy to know Jim understands our culture so well and knew there was only one right choice with this dilemma. It's family first!

When James told me this story, I walked over to Jim and told him thank you. He responded with, "Of course, that's what we do." He gets it.

As long as you are working at a company that shares your core values, you can lead at any level.

Create an Enjoyable Atmosphere

While James's absence technically cost Trinity in the short run, in the big picture scheme of life, Trinity becomes the beneficiary. Think about it. James now knows from firsthand experience that we have his back. We're not just in this game to make a huge profit. We're crafting a culture that cares for people. This creates incredible loyalty. It makes people *want* to go to work. It motivates them to tell others and helps recruit people to our company.

And here is the great news. When your team enjoys showing up for work, there is an amazing transformation that takes place. You shift from a culture of whiners and people who complain about their bosses to a culture of people who are positive and happy to work together. Even when times are tough, they dig deep and expect everyone else to do so as well.

With the way the labor market is today, we as leaders and owners need to do everything in our power to make the workplace a fun, exciting, and engaging place to work. It's our responsibility to build an organization where people want to be. My goal was to be the leader in an inclusive company, and this is how I decided to get there.

That said, if you are fearful of what you are getting yourself into, I understand. This whole process can feel like you're jumping off a bridge into the unknown. But once again, the key is to start small and get some wins under your belt. Create incentives that do not cost that much money and only require a little extra time and energy.

Remember that in the early stages, you're still selling your bosses, your team, and even yourself on whether this will work. But if you can establish some strong wins, you build momentum. Pretty soon, your team starts thinking to themselves, *Hey, if we can hit this target, we can hit an even bigger target!* And so the game begins.

I cannot emphasize enough how important it is to make this process fun. Life is hard, and you want those in your department to show up with an eagerness to grow. There are so many things you can do to foster a sense of healthy camaraderie among groups. You might try making a contest between departments, where the winner takes home bragging rights. I remember several years ago when we had a game where the shop was divided into three sections, and the contest was about who kept their area the cleanest. We took an old golfing trophy of mine and dolled it up. It's funny how something this simple could get guys so excited. They took pride in winning that trophy for the month!

This comes back to the idea that most high-performing people like some competition and enjoy seeing their names posted on the wall. And soon, if everything progresses and management sees the results you generate, it shouldn't be long before they are on board and are willing to put some money behind these games.

Set Expectations and Follow Them

Do not misunderstand what I am saying. I'm not talking about creating a culture that is all fun and games and where no work is accomplished. Unfortunately, some organizations have erred on this way of thinking, and the results have been disastrous.

As Jack Stack says, "I am second to none in believing that business ought to be people oriented. But no company serves its people well by elevating emotions over numbers."[19] There needs to be a set of expectations that people follow, because it is only as you work hard that you can create an enjoyable place for people to work.

As a leader, I have learned from managers on my team. I am a better man because of our interactions. Over time, I have discovered there is a whole lot of give-and-take that needs to go on in hierarchical relationships between a leader and their team.

Personally, I have certain nonnegotiables. I demand clear communication and want everything to be done the proper way by following established procedures. For example, a couple of days ago, before writing this chapter, I was on a call at the beginning of the week with our team. During this conversation, one of our members mentioned we were thinking of purchasing a tractor. I didn't understand all the reasons for this decision and assumed we would circle back to this conversation in future meetings. I had been in every Monday maintenance meeting and hadn't heard it mentioned, and this is the place where that's supposed to take place. All I heard was that we might need another tractor at some point.

To my surprise, several days later I noticed a purchase order for this tractor arrive on my computer, with a request for my approval. Even

---

19 Darren Dahl, "How To Beat The Great Quit: Detoxify Your Workplace Culture," The Great Game of Business, last modified December 7, 2021, https://www.greatgame.com/blog/how-to-beat-the-great-quit-detoxify-your-workplace-culture.

though the price tag was not exactly a huge number for a company of our size, something about the way this had been handled did not sit well with me. For starters, I didn't understand why we needed another tractor to begin with. Also, this tractor was a John Deere, whereas in the past we had purchased only Komatsu tractors and had parts we could swap out between machines if we needed to make quick fixes.

My refusal to approve this order caused a bit of a stir. To be honest, some of my team felt insulted and thought I was trying to micromanage a situation. That day, several of the guys came into my office, and we had a few choice words as I explained my position.

"Guys, I don't care that we're buying a tractor," I said. "I just need to know what we're doing and why we're doing it before I approve something." They vented a few of their frustrations, and we left the subject alone. If they would have brought it up in our standard meeting and had an open discussion, there would have been no issue. But having heard next to nothing about this prior to receiving an invoice bothered me.

That afternoon these same guys came into my office again, and one of them said, "Robert, I want to apologize. We handled this terribly. Even though we think this is a good purchase for our company, we should have gone about this in a different way. We have a system in place to bring up and discuss these kinds of purchases, and we blew it. We're sorry."

> Systems, processes, and discussions are critical to an organization's long-term success. If we ignore them in one area, we will ignore them in other areas.

This acknowledgment got us back on the same page, and after we discussed the benefits of the new tractor, I approved it without hesitation.

I did this not because I wanted to be a jerk or assert a sense of dominance over my team. But systems, processes, and discussions are critical to an organization's long-term success. If we ignore them in one area, we will ignore them in other areas, and this sets a terrible precedent.

As I see it, my role as a leader is to know those nonnegotiables (these are different for each leader and need to be defined) and then leave wiggle room for others to lead. When I know I have someone on my team who fits our company's culture, I do all in my power to keep them around—even if they are not a perfect fit for their current role.

I share this story to hopefully offer a balanced perspective. On one hand, we have stories like James's, where we step in and say, "Family first." But then there are also stories where tough decisions need to be made, leaving room for feelings to be hurt. You need both perspectives to run a healthy organization.

Get People in the Right Seats

As you set expectations and create the culture you want for your team, there will be an inevitable shuffling of the deck. Some of the leaders you thought were in the right seat on the bus need to be shifted to another. And some of the quiet, reserved individuals who have said little until this point might emerge as your greatest superstars.

The key is to find people who fit your organizational values and then find the right seat for them. Paul is a perfect example. He first started working for us back in 2006. The following year I announced to our team that we were going to build a pipe mill, and I asked

Paul if he wanted to help lead the charge. He was excited about this opportunity and liked the idea. There was just one problem. After a few years, I noticed Paul was struggling to manage people. Nothing terrible, but there was enough there that made me realize he was in the wrong role.

At first we let this play out because we were all new at making pipe. But as the team grew larger, it became evident we needed someone with different skills. Still, Paul had the Trinity cultural DNA and possessed an interesting set of skills I knew were valuable, even if I couldn't see the seat on the bus on which he was supposed to sit.

This continued for several years, and I'm sure Paul must have felt some frustration along this journey. But we talked our way through it, and he stuck around. In 2015, we started looking for a maintenance manager because our pipe mill machine was about eight years old, and maintenance was starting to get to be a larger issue.

By this point we were tracking all our downtime and noticed our numbers continued to rise at an alarming rate. Our critical number for downtime was 5 percent or lower, and we were running in the 7 to 10 percent range every week.

At $3,000 per hour of profit and ninety-six hours of operation in a week, 5 percent meant 4.8 hours and $14,400 lost each week due to shutdowns. This alone is a staggering number. But get that number around 10 percent and the amount of potential income lost each year went through the roof.

Initially we hired someone from outside the organization who did not understand our culture. They came in with a "my way or the highway" mentality and ended up rubbing a lot of our guys the wrong way. While he knew the business well, his brash personality drove guys off almost faster than we could hire them. It was obvious he wasn't a fit, and I was glad when another opportunity opened for him to move along to a different company.

When this happened, Paul came to me and said, "Hey, let me be maintenance manager. I already know how all this stuff needs to work." By this point, we had some new preventive maintenance processes in place, and as soon as he came forward with this idea, I knew he had found his fit. It took him ten years to find his role, but now that he has discovered it, he loves what he does and excels in doing it.

As I write this, I peeked at our downtime numbers for this year, and we are hovering under 5 percent (we've even had some weeks of 1 or 2 percent). It's the best it's ever been, and there is no doubt in my mind that Paul is sitting in the right seat.

Another example is a guy named Nick. He was a young, talented drafter. I liked him so much I wanted to make him a scheduler. Unfortunately he worked under someone on our team we had to fire. And during this season, this poor manager had clipped his wings a few times and left Nick feeling demoralized and frustrated with his role.

Sensing his disgruntlement, I invited Nick to my office. When he came in, he had a sour look on his face, and it wasn't hard to sense his mood. "Are you hating me?" I asked him.

He softened and we had a good conversation. "Look, Nick," I said. "You are a talented guy and I want to keep you. I know it feels like you are getting bumped around, and you haven't found the right fit, but I promise you will. Just hang in there, and we will get you in the proper seat."

Long story short, Nick did hang in there and remained part of our team. In fact, the position he holds today places him in a spot where he is driving one of our newest innovations, which I will reference more in chapter 10. Nick has taken this new initiative by the horns and travels with us to meet all our vendors.

I share these stories to offer you a word of hope. It might be you find yourself at odds with your boss. You have one vision, and they have another. If this is where you are, you need to decide whether it's time to move on or to stick around until you find your fit. Sometimes finding ways to implement change takes time.

It could be you are able to make some changes, but you feel frustrated. You like the people on your team, but you don't feel like they are in the right seats on the bus. As a result, making the switch to open-book leadership and implementing continuous improvement feels like a fruitless pursuit. You keep thinking to yourself, *I just need to get everyone situated before I make any major changes.* To a degree, this might be true. But I would encourage you not to wait too long.

As I have shared, there was a great deal of uncertainty when we first implemented the principles outlined in this book. Not everyone was in the right role, and I soon realized some were not a right fit for our team altogether. But instead of waiting around for the perfect time, we pressed forward and grew along the journey.

Build Great Relationships

If you are in a midlevel management position, one of your top goals should be to create as many healthy relationships as possible. I cannot stress this enough. The moment you are hired, start building relationships and networking as early as possible. The connections might not pan out to anything, but leaving a good impression can help even years down the line.

Sometimes even the smallest seeds can produce incredible fruit. Relationships with financial people, employees, customers, and venders are all critical to long-term success. This is the thing about relationships. It's not as if you receive an instant payoff the moment you build a great relationship with a member of your team, but the big picture rewards can be wonderful.

Even as a business owner of an established company, I am constantly planting seeds everywhere I go. From trade shows to one-on-one interactions, I am speaking with people about our company. Hey, it's why I included our company phone number in a previous chapter! Bottom line: if you are a great person who shares our organization's values, I want you on our team. That is the way I think.

When you have a good company culture, people are attracted to you. I look at building relationships with others the same way I view investing. You might place only a couple of dollars in the bank, but over time the interest begins to accumulate. And like business, there have been times I have taken a leap of faith and invested in someone who might have appeared as a risky proposition to others. However, sometimes it's the "risky" investments that offer the highest returns. Sometimes all people need is an opportunity.

To me, this just makes so much sense, and I do not understand why every business doesn't run their company this way.

Consistency over Time

The beauty of making wise decisions is that your good choices compound over time. In *The Compound Effect*, Darren Hardy writes, "It's not the big things that add up in the end; it's the hundreds, thousands, or millions of little things that separate the ordinary from the extraordinary."[20]

---

20 Darren Hardy, *The Compound Effect: Jumpstart Your Income, Your Life, Your Success* (Bhopal, India: Manjul Publishing, 2012).

Trinity was far from an overnight success. It took us decades of trial and error to get where we are. But those small decisions I made in the 1990s are paying huge dividends today. This was something Jack Stack told me would happen, but it was not a statement I thoroughly believed would prove true.

To me, it all boils down to consistency over time. Learn what works best and keep making right decisions over and repeatedly. John Maxwell writes, "I've long been a fan of consistency. In fact, it's one of the subjects I'm most passionate about when it comes to the subjects of leadership and personal growth because in both arenas, consistency is the key to success. When you start something, work daily at getting better at it, and stick with it over time, you'll see a return on your investment greater than anything you could've imagined."[21]

Everyone wants to know how to be an instant success. I get it. But success does not happen in an instant. It takes years of development and personal determination. And even those few individuals who quickly strike it rich often falter as the years progress. They achieved great wealth, but they did not have the character to match their achievements.

I love Napoleon Hill's Eleven Major Attributes of Leadership:

1. **Unwavering Courage:** This means full belief in oneself and one's occupation. No intelligent follower will follow a leader who lacks self-confidence and courage.

2. **Self-Control:** If you cannot control yourself, then you can never control others. Self-control is a must in leadership!

3. **A Keen Sense of Justice:** Essential for leadership in any calling. Otherwise you will lose the respect of your followers.

---

21   John Maxwell, "2020: A Year of Pioneers and Investors," January 2, 2020, https://www.johnmaxwell.com/blog/2020-a-year-of-pioneers-and-investors.

4. **Definiteness of Decision:** If you do not make strong decisions, then you are unsure. People do not follow one who is unsure.

5. **Definiteness of Plans:** You must plan your work and work your plan. Otherwise you are moving by guesswork and will eventually fail.

6. **The Habit of Doing More Than Paid For:** Hill found that all leaders who succeed in an outstanding way are always willing to do more than they require from their followers.

7. **A Pleasing Personality:** This is needed to get the respect of followers (whether they be customers, workers, or shareholders) and is essential.

8. **Sympathy and Understanding:** A successful leader must be in sympathy with his or her followers and understand their problems.

9. **Mastery of Details:** All great leaders know every single detail of their position to the most minute detail. They master whatever is expected of them.

10. **Willingness to Assume Full Responsibility:** A successful leader must be willing to be responsible for the mistakes and shortcomings of their followers.

11. **Cooperation:** This is essential. As well as cooperating with others, a successful leader must also induce his or her followers to cooperate. Leadership calls for power, and power is only available through the help of others, which requires cooperation.

Bottom line: work on these traits and you will win. Be the individual or company that develops the habit of doing what you least like to do and the ability to do it when you least want to do it.

When you possess these attributes and live them out well over years and years of service to others, you can make an extraordinary impact.

An Open-Door Policy

As an owner I have an open-door policy that anyone can come in and talk. My managers know I have their backs and that I will not take anything I hear on just face value. They know that we at Trinity only want to get better and that part of this requires being able to hear from people at all levels.

If you are a midlevel manager in an organization, I encourage you to lead with a sense of openness. Operate in such a way that people trust you and feel free to bring their challenges to you.

Remember, if you work at an organization that likes this self-defeating language, you are probably in the wrong place. Statements like, "Because I said so!" or "Because we've always done it that way" or "Because I'm the boss!" all undermine your ability to lead at a high level.

Many times, when people come into my office, they have problems that fall outside of work. They need help or coaching in other areas of their lives. Regardless, whenever they start talking, I listen and take notes.

If you are a midlevel manager, do not underestimate your ability to influence change.

Initially, this open-door policy created uncertainty with some of my managers. They feared I might undercut them or take their team members' word at face value. But over time I have earned their trust through being fair.

I share this to challenge you. If you are a midlevel manager, do not underestimate your ability to influence change. Allow people the freedom to speak their minds. Build strong relationships. Set manageable expectations. And do the right thing consistently over time. This is how I would encourage you to lead, regardless of your level.

Takeaways

➡ Family comes first.

➡ Successful people develop the habits to do what they least like to do when they least want to do it!

➡ As a manager and leader, think about the ways open-book leadership and continuous improvement can benefit you and your company.

➡ What leadership qualities do you think make you worth following?

➡ What could you change or improve to be a better leader?

➡ What types of qualities do *you* expect in leaders? Have you told your employees in leadership roles what you expect from them? Are they listed out clearly?

➡ Would you feel comfortable training someone to do your job?

➡ Do you have a plan on how you could make your department better? Creating a list and addressing the issues one by one will help immensely. Even creating games to work toward that goal will help.

➡ Regarding games—think of some ways to make work fun! How can you improve employees' fun in the office?

➡ Think of some standard meeting processes and rules that you follow and write them out.

➡ Do you have employees who aren't in the right seat on the bus? Would you be able to move them? For those who have left, how were your discussions with them before they exited?

➡ Think about your work culture and how you could change it for the better each and every day.

➡ Do you work on your work relationships every day? Remember, you are always selling!

➡ How consistent have you been with your daily decisions? Consistency is key!

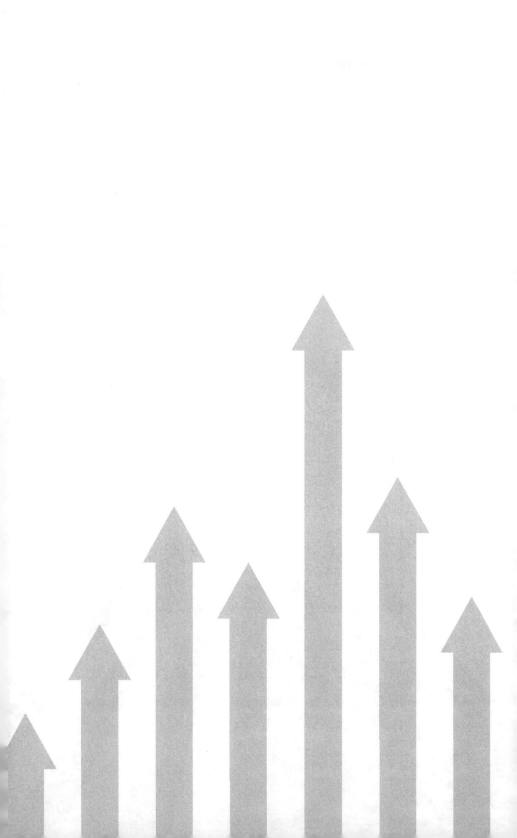

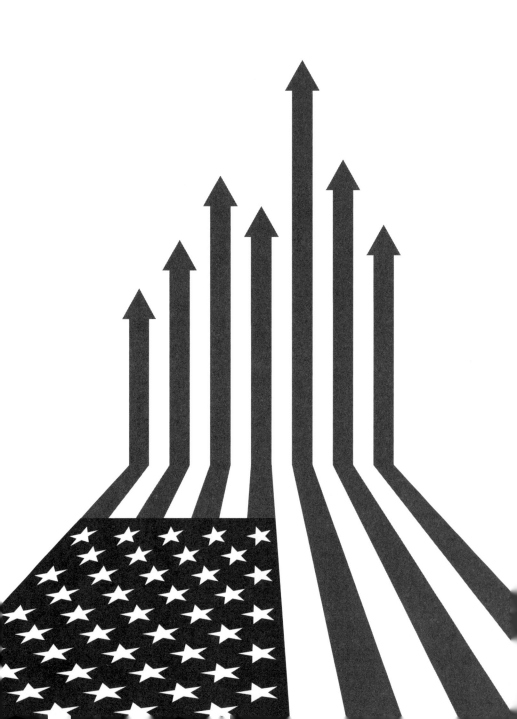

CHAPTER 9

CASHING OUT

It's easy to get into business, but it's much tougher to get out. I share this from personal experience.

From my standpoint, there are two types of businesses. The first is where you do all you can to harvest cash. You're not looking to necessarily build a brand to hand on to someone else. Instead, the goal is to make as much money as possible while you are in, invest the revenue generated, and hope for the best when it is time to sell.

Businesses in this category often range from below $1 million to as much as $20 million in value. As Jack Stack often says, this is when entrepreneurs stop growing, because they can no longer control everything. But it's at this point they usually hit a wall. This is where either the business stops growing or is acquired by a larger company. Owners start to grow frustrated because they cannot control everything themselves, and they make the startling realization that *they* are the business. And because this approach tends to be more "mom and pop" in style, there are not as many systems in place that allow the business to function well if the one person at the top is no longer around. As a result, these companies are tougher to sell.

The second form of business is one where your goal becomes to create the most value. Many times this happens organically and usually means sacrificing your initial payday and reinvesting the earnings you make back into the organization.

Both approaches can prove successful if implemented in the right way. The key is to know what path is right for you and stick with it. Personally, I bet on our team and landed on the second option.

While other owners of steel companies harvested cash along their journey, I continued to reinvest the funds I had back into the company. Admittedly, in some ways this was riskier, and I can see why some would not go this route. Many owners I spoke with were content to take a nice salary, join a local country club, put their kids through college, and live a nice life. There is nothing wrong with this approach. But for me, I knew I wanted to build something special, and this drove me to continue to reinvest.

Admittedly, this was a tougher position to take in the first few years of Trinity's operation. Even though I was making a nice income, there were points when it would have been nice to pull out the extra cash we were generating and use it for our family. But year after year, I continued to reinvest our company's earnings back into the growth and development of our business. And all these years later, I'm glad I made this decision.

When you choose this path, it can take some time to gain traction. At this point, you might take out a few bank loans, start to develop traction, and keep your overhead low. The goal is to develop a sustained pace. You do not want to be exposed to a lot of risk. When I chose this route, it allowed me to create the business I envisioned, but it also caused the need for a liquidity event when it was time to get out, forcing me to be at the mercy of the marketplace economy at the time it needed to happen.

In other words, I took a calculated risk. Yes, there was a chance my business could have gone under, and I would have lost most of my assets, but I believed in what I was doing. Unlike other owners, I never used Trinity as a personal piggy bank. If I flew out to California for a two-day business trip but stayed a week, I spent those five extra days on my dime. Doing so set a precedent for my managers and helped me create the culture I wanted to create.

I was not risk averse and was willing to spend money on new equipment, buildings, or people.

Eventually, one of the most frequent compliments I heard about Trinity from my peers was that we were a business that could be acquired or become an employee stock ownership plan (ESOP) business. Because of the systems we had in place, we were not a one-man show.

Through these conversations, we started talking about the possibility of ESOPs. Before these conversations, I had heard of ESOPs, but I didn't know that much about them. It was something Jack Stack had talked about and was part of their ownership structure, so I figured it might be a great option.

What compelled me to create an ESOP was the same thing that drove me to open-book leadership. I loved the concept of spreading the profits—and the responsibility. It just made so much sense to have someone involved in the game.

TRINITY ESOP PLAN VALUE

	ACTUAL 12/31/2019	ACTUAL 12/31/2020	ACTUAL 12/31/2021
TOTAL ALL COMPANY SHARES			
Total # Shares	197,375	197,375	197,375
Value per Share	$35.08	$49.81 (1)	$222.00 (2)
Total Share Value	$6,923,915	$9,831,249	$43,817,250
COMPANY SHARES DISTRIBUTED TO PARTICIPANTS			
Total # Shares Distributed	9,793	6,425	7,651
Value Shares Distributed	$343,536	$320,029	$1,698,539
% of Total	4.96%	3.26%	3.88%
CUMMULATIVE COMPANY SHARES DISTRIBUTED TO PARTICIPANTS			
# Shares Distributed	9,793	16,218	23,869
Value Shares Distributed	$343,536	$807,815	$5,298,918
% of Total	4.96%	8.22%	12.09%
# of ESOP Participants	128	126	137
Average Balance per Participant	$2,684	$6,411	$38,678

NOTES:
(1) 42% increase in share price
(2) 346% increase from 2020, 533% from 2019

Creating an Employee Stock Ownership Plan

The rollout of our ESOP plan for Trinity occurred in 2019. By this point I knew I needed a way out as sole owner of the company. I still enjoyed going to work each day, but there was always the pressure that maybe I would not receive the financial windfall I hoped to receive.

Originally we pursued having another company buy us out and went through the traditional process of having our company evaluated and scrutinized. But the more our team talked, the more we realized the concept of an ESOP fit our culture and made so much financial sense.

An ESOP is a lot like a 401(k). The US government allows you to sell your stock to a trust in which all the employees receive shares over a predetermined period—ours is thirty years. The beauty of this is our new company did not have to pay federal or state taxes.

The history of ESOPs dates back several decades to a point when the federal government wanted to encourage employers to allow their employees to have a stake in their company.

So imagine your company sold $10 million, had 5 percent net return on sales, and made $500,000 in profit. Assuming you lived in Missouri, you would pay as high as 35 percent in federal taxes and 7 percent in state taxes—bringing the grand total to 42 percent of your profits out the door. This means that out of your $500,000 in profit, you now have only $290,000 remaining. It was this understanding that made an ESOP so attractive.

This is significant, to say the least, and allows the new ESOP to have the cash to pay for your shares you sold the trust. And these funds are then used to pay the owner who sold his shares to the trust.

Again, the purpose of this is to help everyone in the company think like an owner. This is the secret to sustainable success. Whenever employees have skin in the game, that changes the way they approach everything.

When this happens, there are so many wins. You end up with a smart, fully educated, engaged workforce. You have a system in place to cultivate your own leaders—the hardest commodity to find in business today. You have a fully functioning system of self-improvement that will keep your business getting better forever. And you have given them a way to be owners in something they helped create. You've given yourself a way to sell your business at close to its max value without much risk. And you've made the lives and future of every

> **ESOPs run hand in glove with open-book leadership.**

employee better, as they have a chance to own shares in something they work at every day.

ESOPs run hand in glove with open-book leadership. Once employees are invested in the company, they have this tremendous sense of ownership. As they see their shares go up or down, they have an even greater realization that what they do matters. And even when they go down, they learn that things happen, and we must be always present to get ahead.

While the process of establishing this type of company was time consuming and had its challenges, the benefits are that our company is sustainable.

Again, it's not as if I started with this grand plan in mind to take our business to where it is today. Initially, all I thought about was survival and ways to make my life easier. But as I and our company continue to mature, scalability remains something that is important to me.

Everyone Is Different

That said, it bears repeating that this approach is not for everyone. For instance, I was in California this one time when I was talking with a person whose father-in-law owned a photography studio. As this older gentleman was passing away, he turned to my friend and said, "Listen, I need you to pay attention. If something happens to me, I want you to go to a board in my office and pull it down. Behind this board is a note." At this point my friend was thinking to himself, *What in the world is going on?*

Dutifully obeying his instructions, he went to the board and pulled it down. And to his amazement, there was a safe behind the board that contained $37,000 in twenty-dollar bills!

As I listened to this story, I thought to myself, *Here was a guy who was probably weary of an economic depression and wanted to make sure he had enough saved for a rainy day.* For him, the peace of mind he gained by having $37,000 stuffed away in his wall outweighed what he could have received if he'd reinvested that money back in his company, in the bank, or in the stock market. Sure, he might have quadrupled his investment if he had invested it properly, but every business owner is different.

The reality is there is not one correct way to do business. If you are an owner and want to take 10 percent of your company's earnings each year and invest them in the stock market, that's fine. This is just a different picture from the one I had, but it's still a great plan.

And even though I think ESOPs are fantastic, not every company will experience the immediate success we have had. Just the other day, I was speaking with a friend who created an ESOP, but then COVID-19 hit. When that happened, his company's shares went down and put a dent in his bottom line.

At the end of the day, every business owner must determine what level of risk they want to run, with the understanding their business could become obsolete within a few short years. When you consider IBM fax machines, Kodak cameras, Blackberry smartphones, and shopping mall owners, there is the ever-present realization that what works one day might be a thing of the past tomorrow.

During those days I reinvested most of our earnings back in the company, my wife would sometimes stop me and say, "Why are we making this purchase for the business when we could be saving or investing it somewhere else?" My response was this: "Because it's the right thing to do." Fortunately, I am blessed with a great wife, and this always satisfied her. She believed in me, and that fueled my motivation.

Plan with Caution

I say all this with an added word of warning. If you are like me and prioritize your business above other forms of investment or savings, I caution you to make sure you are always realistic. Sometimes I have watched owners constantly reinvest in their businesses and do so with a naive perception of what their business is worth. They might go years without harvesting any cash, and in the end they wind up with a business that is worth less than they think it's worth.

For example, I had a local pipe guy in St. Louis who had been in business about five years longer than us. He made the statement to me, "We don't make a lot of money, but we always make money!" Reading between the lines, I realized he was counting on the big payday he believes will come down the road. However, only the market will determine whether this will prove accurate.

While I hate to be the bearer of bad news, this is an important reality to address. It's seldom that what an owner thinks their company is worth matches that of the person who will write them the check. This should come as no surprise. From the purchaser's perspective, it is their job to pick companies apart and buy them for the lowest price possible. This is not wrong, and each of us would do the same thing if we were placed in this position. I say this to challenge you to not get your head in the clouds and assume some larger company will sweep you off your feet with a truckload of cash.

There is an even more morbid outcome on the table. Let's say, God forbid, a business owner does not put their company in order, and they pass away. Often the result is that vultures swoop in and pilfer the company—leaving the family in a terrible position. I've seen this happen more than once, and it's devastating.

This is why twenty years ago I created a succession plan called, "What happens when Robert gets hit by a beer truck on the way to work." Through injecting a bit of humor, I covered a worst-case situation and outlined what our leadership would do if such an event occurred. To me, this was the right thing to do. It gave my family peace of mind and created a sense of stability in our organization. That way workers wouldn't have to constantly wonder what might happen if I was no longer around.

I sat down with my management group, and we wrote out a plan. We made sure we had enough insurance on me and my partner so that no one would have to panic if something bad happened. We wrote out who would take what roles and who would call the bank and our major vendors if I was not around. We included our bank in this conversation and shared with our major vendors that we had a succession plan in case of emergency.

We developed a plan to have extra cash in place so my family would not have to dip into personal savings to keep the company afloat. The last thing I wanted was for my family to go bankrupt to "honor Robert's legacy" through keeping his business alive.

After creating this succession plan, we took the time to read it in front of our entire company twice a year. "All right, folks, it's time to read 'What happens when Robert gets hit by a beer truck on the way to work.'" The room would erupt with laughter, and then we would

> **If you are a leader, you need to have a succession plan in place.**

get down to business. During these times, I made sure my wife, Shelly, attended the meetings so that she was kept in the loop.

If you are a leader, you need to have a succession plan in place. Even if you are a small organization, make sure you are insured with more insurance than you need—preferably on a twenty-year term. Always think of the worst-case scenario and prepare for what should happen when you are no longer able to operate.

Presenting ESOP to Our Team

When I presented the ESOP concept to our employees, it made immediate sense to them. Even though some of the details were tough to understand, the overarching concept connected. And so we established a number for the sale of the company. Then we instituted a plan for company employees to buy me out.

In simple terms, it's a bit like paying down the principal of a home. If your mortgage is $100,000 and you pay off $10,000 in one year, that is $10,000 that is in your pocket should you ever resell the home. Along the way, you have hopefully gained equity in the home, creating an additional stream of revenue that will pay off in the future.

During the first two years of our ESOP, we distributed over sixteen thousand shares of Trinity stock to Trinity employees, valued at over $800,000. With 126 employees, the average balance per employee as of December 31, 2020, was over $6,400. In 2021, we distributed shares of stock valued at over five million with an average balance per employee (based on salary) of $39,000. And this was at zero cost and risk to the employees.

Our employees are eligible to participate in the ESOP after twelve months of continuous employment from their hire date. If they have worked at least one thousand hours in those twelve months, they automatically become eligible. Employees become ESOP participants the first January 1 or July 1 after becoming eligible. Trinity stock shares are allocated to active participants each December 31. If they become an

ESOP participant on July 1 of any given year, they receive 50 percent (a half year) of their full stock allocation that first year of participation.

Statements are mailed to their home the July following the date stock shares are allocated. ESOP participants become fully vested after completion of three years of employment. Termination of employment before reaching three years results in forfeiture of all stock shares.

In years 2019–21, our employees made out better than all of us could have imagined. We had great years, and this has created an additional buzz among the team. Just the other day, I heard one of our guys had a BBQ at his home. When he began sharing the details of our ESOP, his neighbor wanted to join and asked if he could get an interview. These stories are not uncommon, and we often have people saying, "Hey, would you hire my relative or friend?"

It's funny, because those monthly slips of paper that show the ebbs and flows of the company did more for collective buy-in than any words I could have given.

Open-book leadership, continuous improvement, and ESOPs are the three-headed monster for success. When you have the first two, the last step is a no-brainer.

Create the Culture You Want

If you are not an owner, but you work as a manager for a company that is in the midst of creating an ESOP, this should get you excited. If you believe in your company, this will give you a fresh opportunity.

As an owner, I am beyond excited at the ways I see our culture continuing to grow. As this has happened, I've found outsiders admire what we've accomplished. Talented, honest, hardworking, sharing, optimistic, caring people like being around similar people. Remember, like attracts like. People gravitate to what is good. Trinity now feels like we are a magnet for quality customers, vendors, and good people. We're not an organization based on one person. We are a team.

During the pandemic we have had several situations arise that have benefited the whole Trinity team. Around February 2020, we received a call from a plate vendor that we purchased about $5 to $10 million of plate from a year. He contacted our Bryan Davis, vice president at Trinity. Bryan had started at Trinity in 2000 in the accounting department, moved to scheduling the mill, then became our sales manager—an outside-the-box move, but I wanted someone to build a system and not just close deals for people. (Also, a word to the wise: for some reason companies always make the best salesperson the sales manager, but that person just ends up closing orders for people because he's great at one thing—selling! It's better to build a sales system and get organized.)

Anyway, Bryan spoke with his friend Chad. And as Chad shared, even though he had been a successful sales manager, a twenty-year employee of his company, and instrumental in their leap from $20 million to $700 million in sales, he was asked to leave.

Long story short, their culture had changed and become more and more corporate. Somewhere along the line, this organization lost its way and did not place a premium on sales as they had in the past. I believe they assumed sales was easy and asked Chad to make cuts to the sales commissions and department head count because of COVID-19. He wanted to wait and better see the full impact the pandemic might have on their company.

Because they came to an impasse, Chad was asked to leave, and he decided to launch a new company that would have the same values as when he'd first started. He had come up with three potential partners: a venture capital group, another company, and Trinity.

Despite being in a pandemic, I remembered my "Griggs Rule" that says opportunity only happens when you are least prepared to take advantage of it. And so, as the world shut down, my team met with Chad's new leadership team, and they pitched us on the future of their business. Because of where we were in our company's trajectory, our team felt like a plate division would be a perfect add-on to our pipe manufacturing and fabrication.

Jim Nazzoli, our chief operating officer (COO), and Jason Perry, our CFO, felt like the downside was low and the upside was great. Essentially, it was a total distribution operation that took prime plates, cut them, and loaded them on a truck. This was something we had actually done at Trinity thirteen years earlier with pipe but had since shifted our focus into manufacturing. Bottom line: we knew how this space worked and understood the value Chad's new company could offer.

Now for the great part! We sold and shipped our first plates in July 2020. As of October 2021, they have sold thirty-eight thousand tons of plate for over $50 million! We have opened three locations: our first in northern Indiana; a second in Philadelphia, Pennsylvania, at our transloading facility; and one in Kansas City, with two more locations coming in the next year.

This great opportunity happened only because the people we were close to thought we had a great culture and they wanted to be part of it. And this is just one of several situations that have come about this year.

The point is that opportunity favors the courageous. If you sit back and always play it safe, you might be able to earn a decent living. But if you really go for it, you will be able to build a company and culture that people are proud to be a part of—and makes you a ton of money in the process!

Takeaways

➡ Do you have a business … or are you a business?

    ▫ If you *are* a business, do you have a written succession plan?

➡ Ask your management team if they know who they are and how their role operates within the business. What would they do if something happened to you? Your management team should understand how the business operates and should be able to "run" the business.

➡ Have you spoken with your bank and major vendors should something happen to you at the head of your business? How about your family?

➡ Think about how you could exit your business. It's never too early to have a plan.

➡ How would ESOPs increase the value of your business and allow you to be a built-in purchaser?

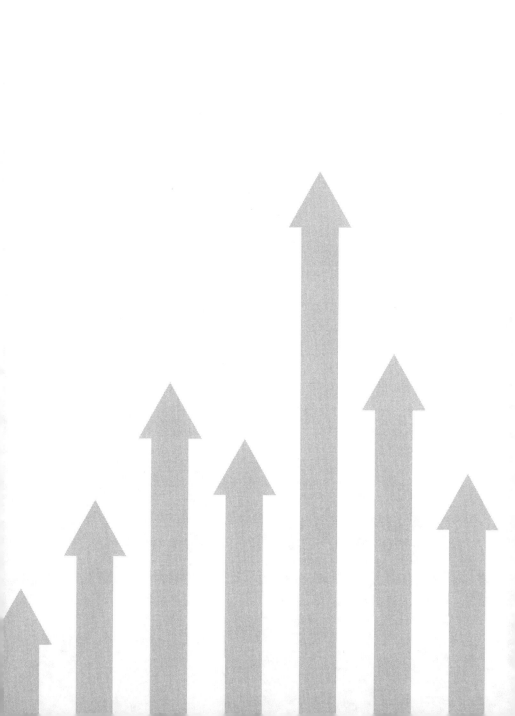

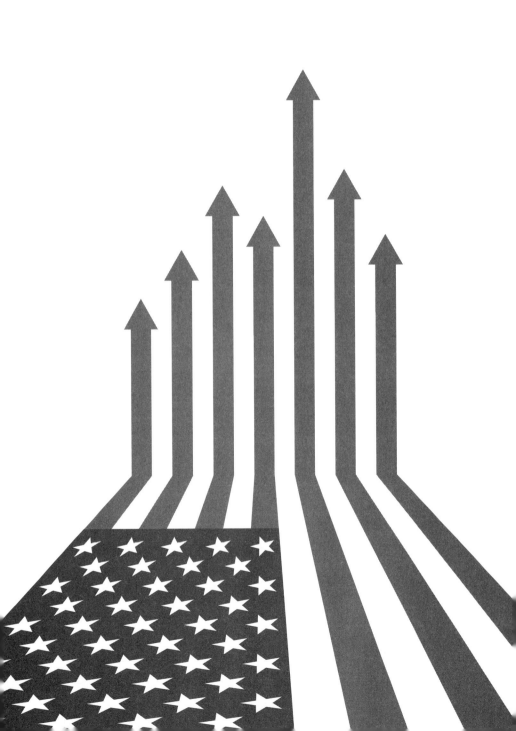

CHAPTER 10

STAY HUNGRY

If there is one piece of advice I would leave you with as we conclude, it would be this: stay hungry.

Unfortunately, as time goes by and you experience success, it's easy to become complacent. You lose that drive to succeed and do processes well. When this happens, you settle for less than what your company could be, and it is only a matter of time before other organizations are hot on your trail.

The secret of my success at Trinity is not much of a secret. It is getting up and doing the right thing every single day. For the first twenty years of our existence, in an era when cell phones were not readily available to the public, I was at my desk every morning at 7:30 a.m. to answer the phone. For me, my office

> The secret of my success at Trinity is not much of a secret. It is getting up and doing the right thing every single day.

was Grand Central Station. If I became complacent and started to slack, I might have missed out on a deal that might change the future of our company.

Success is all about doing the little things well every day. It's showing up when you say you will show up. It's being a person of your word. It's saying no to complacency and choosing to stay motivated through good and hard times. And it's being humble enough to admit when you are wrong and looking for ways to grow as a person.

Let's look at a specific illustration that is unfolding as I close out this book.

The Story of Tri-Loc

The history of American innovation usually tells a tale of three innovators who have a similar story, with only one prevailing. Such was the case with an innovation called Permalok.

Tri-Loc is Trinity's version, and it is a weldless interlocking system that creates a cost-effective method for pipe installation while also improving jobsite efficiencies. Essentially, our Tri-Loc utilizes a precision-machined slip joint fit that eliminates the need for time-intensive field-applied butt welds on casing pipe installations.

It's a bit like walking into Home Depot and seeing SharkBite plumbing connections for your home. Because this click-and-go solution is user friendly and does not require installers to be professional welders, it becomes a great alternative for do-it-yourselfers. This is a simplified version of what Tri-Loc does.

Because our spiral-welded pipe is manufactured from hot-rolled coil rather than steel plate rolled into pipe cans one plate at a time (also called rolled-and-welded pipe and the type Permalok used), spiral-welded pipe saves customers an average of 10 percent a ton in raw material costs. This process allows our mill to run any length of pipe without waste and minimizes the shutdown time for welding. This means we can manufacture four to five thousand tons per month as compared to the five hundred tons per month on average at a rolled-and-welded shop, with roughly the same amount of people.

As a result, customers have shorter lead times and more material available to them with our spiral-welded pipe. In the field, no welding results in huge savings for the customer. This reduces expenses for labor, equipment, and travel and means many projects can now be completed in half the time. Just last week a new customer used our thirty-six-inch Tri-Loc in New Jersey and installed 180 feet of pipe in less than a day. If this same project required welding, it would have added an additional day or two to this time frame.

Tri-Loc is an incredible system that is more user friendly than any other product on the market. Besides this reality, Tri-Loc can be a huge moneymaker. For every truckload of pipe off our mill, we make about a 35 percent profit margin. But if we sell a truckload of Tri-Loc, we end up with roughly a 50 percent margin. Observing the differences between these two systems, I believed our method would be a huge advantage when we went to compete with Permalok after their patent expired.

Now here is the interesting part. Permalok had been around for decades. However, the way it was produced and marketed targeted larger companies that used larger quantities and did micro tunneling. Rather than improving this technology and making it more accessible and user friendly for other markets, they continued to send out the same product that had earned them a modest profit for decades. Contrast this with the approach we took.

As soon as their patent expired, we went into the marketplace and asked what consumers wanted. It was clear to me Tri-Loc was the answer. These conversations resulted in us making changes that grew a product that didn't even exist to $7 to $10 million in market sales this year. We took a product that had been around for years, incorporated some innovations, and reached a whole different market.

Now that Trinity has become a player in this industry, I am convinced we know exactly what to do to make this product an even greater success. In fact, within a few years, not only do I expect this product to be the most profitable product line in the history of our company, but I expect it to dictate the way larger thick pipe is put together in the United States!

This didn't come through reinventing the wheel and coming up with a product that was entirely unique from anything that had ever been done. It came through the concept of continuous improvement. It came through looking at what was currently being done, asking the end user questions, and figuring out whether there was a better way to operate.

I Am Still Learning

I write this not to set myself up as some ingenious rock star. Quite the opposite, in fact. Just like you, I have moments when I feel in over my head and don't know what I'm doing.

Take Tri-Loc, for example. Even as I finished the last section of this chapter, something happened to me that made me pause. It reminded me that forty-two years into this journey of leadership, I'm still needing to grow.

It all started five years ago when Permalok's patent expired. The days after this was scheduled to happen, I planned to start work on introducing our own version of this technology. From my estimation, it would be an easy sell. The product had been around for twenty-five years and just needed some improvements. Because we were an established company with a strong reputation, we could lean on our history to enter this new market.

I took this project on personally and picked a team of young employees who were excited about this technology. It was so important to me that I worked on every facet of the business, including marketing, calling customers, meeting people in person, and collecting feedback. I understood the value and market potential and knew we had a winner. Being hands on was important to me because I knew this product would be a game changer. For years, we worked to develop this technology. We applied for and were granted a patent. From here, I thought it was all downhill.

Unfortunately, I misjudged people's reluctance to change. Because we produced this pipe using the spiral-weld I explained earlier, I thought the huge cost savings customers experienced would make them want to switch over to us. But I was wrong. Because we were using a newer, unproven approach, the competition used that against us, and customers only leveraged our lower costs to get our competitor to lower their prices.

So, for the last five years, my team and I traveled all over the United States. We attended every possible convention or trade show you could imagine. And gradually we started to crack the code, winning smaller jobs and proving our process worked with one customer at a time.

Admittedly, I thought this process would go much faster. One year I would project $5 million in sales, and we wouldn't even come close. But at the end of 2020, things started to fall into place. And by the close of 2021 we are on pace to hit $10 million in annual sales. Once again, everything seemed to be trending in the right direction. Then heartbreak struck.

We sold some Tri-Loc to a customer who really liked us. It was a nice order that went well, and they decided to follow it up with a larger one in the $500,000 neighborhood. I was confident our team was up for the challenge and had no fear the work wouldn't go as expected.

But after our delivery, we received a call from this company, letting us know there was an issue. The ends weren't lining up as they should have. And so a few of us flew out to where this company was located to assess the situation. Sure enough, some of the ends were off. This prompted us to write an NCR and launch a PIT.

The first problem was obvious. We fabricated this material then at a different plant, where we normally did large pipes that were sixty inches and above. As a result, our workers operated without the best tools for these large diameters and did their best to improvise. In retrospect, it was a poor decision and one I am frustrated we made at our company's stage of development.

As I write this chapter, this issue has been going on for over two weeks. Recently, I received the full nonconformance report and realize the mess-up was solely our own doing. When I received this call, my initial reaction was anger. I wanted someone's head delivered to me on a platter! I had poured my heart and soul into Tri-Loc, and it was my baby!

All I could think about was what a waste the last five years had been. Because the steel community is a tight-knit group, I knew this company would talk about their experience with us. And those same people I'd spent years selling at trade shows would have to receive a fresh sales pitch whereby I could regain their trust.

But the more I thought about it, the more I realized *I* was the one to blame. It was my responsibility to set procedures, processes, and tools in place at our manufacturing locations. It was my fault these procedures didn't become the standard operating procedure at these facilities. And it was my fault Trinity will lose potentially millions of dollars in new clients from this major mishap.

And so, after a long, sleepless night, I had to make the decision to get back on the horse that just threw me for a loop and keep riding. The more I think about it, I really have so much to be thankful for. I have a great team of people who are committed and love what they do.

Rather than wasting valuable time sulking and feeling sorry for myself, I decided it was time to dust myself off and move on. This meant contacting the customer we wronged, ensuring them we would make it right, and jokingly reminding them that my best customers have come from my biggest mistakes!

Here is another interesting point: not only did I not cast the blame on my team, but they did not get angry with me. Even though they had every right to be frustrated and disappointed with how I had failed them, my team of leaders all took their share of the blame, and we all stuck with each other and owned our mistake together.

When we talk about this whole concept of continuous improvement, one of the ways I know we are on the right track is the way our team responds to adversity. Rather than pointing fingers and throwing others under the bus, we work together to find a resolution.

The continuous improvement journey never stops.

The Beauty of Low Turnover

When you have a team of people who know and like each other, it is no surprise that the turnover of the organization begins to decrease.

At Trinity, we have almost no turnover in our office personnel. People on our sales teams and in administration do not want to go somewhere else, because they love where they are. Phyllis MacConnell, whom I mentioned earlier, was our first employee and has been here forty-two years. Kristy Pride is in HR and has been here over twenty years. Bryan Davis is also over twenty years and is slotted to take my place as president and CEO of Trinity. Buddy Sumpter is the sales manager and has been here over ten years. Ryan Hoffman started at the shipping desk at the mill, and fifteen years later he is now the purchasing manager. Jim Nazzoli, our first real accountant, has been with us for thirteen years. Jason Perry has been with us ten years and is now our CFO. And we have five sales folks with over ten years' experience.

Even in our shop, where the work is hard and turnover is higher, we have people who have stuck around. Paul Wilkerson has been with us for twelve years and serves as the head of maintenance. Coming in the same time as Paul, Evan Hauer now serves as the head of mill operations. Kevin Henry and Drew Blevins started fifteen years ago and continue to work on the quality control side of things. This says something to me. It tells me people genuinely like where they are.

All these names underscore the importance of hiring the right people. When you do, life is so much easier. But the key is to create an environment where the right type of people will want to stick around. You can hire all the talented and resourceful people you can find, but if they do not enjoy where they work, they will soon move along to another organization.

Over the years, we have created different T-shirts for our teams to wear. One of them says, "There's no crying in the steel business." Another says, "We roll the good stuff," and a third says, "I own this place." This last slogan represents the way I want our employees to feel about Trinity. Together we run and own this business. Sure, I might be the guy at the top of the org chart and make some of the top decisions. But my success is dependent on every member of our team, just as their success is reliant on the decisions I make.

To me, every person on the Trinity team is like an extended family member.

Recently I received an email from a team member who shared some fascinating statistics with me.

Of the sixteen members who make up the three divisions of our board of directors, senior management group, and production department managers, the average age is 41.6, and the average length of time at Trinity is 12.3 years.

Aside from our IT department, all our current leadership positions are homegrown. And as this has happened, we have tripled in size from $100 million to $300 million in 2022, so this tells you a lot about the kind of people on our team. Most of them started very early at Trinity and never worked for a large company, so we must be doing something right!

> To me, every person on the Trinity team is like an extended family member.

Engagement in the Process

One of the ways I know others have bought into this mindset is through their engagement in the process. Let me provide an illustration.

Several years ago, another company (which we have since overtaken in size) considered buying us out. They were great at building wealth and were one of the most prosperous steel companies in the nation. Unfortunately, they tended to have a very low view of customers and seemed to forget whom they worked for.

Back in the day, they were the gold standard for structural pipe in the construction industry. Their sales team was great, and I admired the way they ran their business. We were a customer and sold them pipe from our days in distribution.

Gradually, they started to acquire small spiral pipe mills and had them in three locations. As this happened, we started buying from them and had them convert coils to pipe for us. They were predominantly in the piling market, which meant their customers installed pipe vertically, whereas we were in the horizontal market with customers that augered pipe or bored under highways. While we didn't cross paths much, I admired their company from afar. I would bump into them at trade conferences and could tell they were great people who really cared about what they did.

Fast-forward a few years, and they were bought out by a larger steel company that was the gorilla of the steel industry. Unfortunately they were about as arrogant as it got. Long gone were the days when they cared for their customers, and everything they did reeked of big corporate America. Soon after this buyout, we received word that this new company would no longer convert coils for us. Despite being one of their largest clients, they saw us as a threat.

Fortunately I had anticipated a day like this might come. Going back to the days I had seen large companies like Valley Steel fold overnight, I knew it was important to control as many parts of the business as possible. So, in preparation for this day, I had already begun working on plans for a pipe mill that I had in my back pocket. Given the fact we bought more pipe from them than they converted into pipe, I knew they could not afford to cut us off in a second and knew we had about six months to a year to find an alternative. (This is a reminder to always stay ahead of the game and anticipate the worst possible outcomes. It's remembering that "Griggs Rule" that says opportunity or bad situations always come when you can least afford them.)

The moment I realized we were in an untenable position I walked into my partner Vince's office and shared the news. The year was 2006, I was fifty years of age, and we were on the eve of a great recession. I told him we needed to build the mill.

⚜ Trinity Products, Inc.

Prospectus for Proposed Spiral Weld Steel Mill

Production (in Tons)	500	600	700	800	900
Revenue (200 tons @ 420/ton Remaining @ 460/ton)	222,000	268,000	314,000	360,000	406,000
Cost of Sales (200 tons @ 220/ton Remaining @ 300/ton)	134,000	164,000	194,000	224,000	254,000
Gross Profit	88,000	104,000	120,000	136,000	152,000
Expenses					
Labor (no 2nd shift) (See Labor Detail) w/2nd shift	20,860	20,860	20,860	20,860 6,680	20,860 6,680
Sales Department	10,000	10,000	10,000	10,000	10,000
Welding Supplies	9,800	9,800	9,800	12,600	12,600
Gases	750	750	750	1,000	1,000
Repair	2,500	2,500	2,500	5,000	5,000
Utilities	3,000	3,000	3,000	5,000	5,000
Auto	500	500	500	500	500
Insurance	1,000	1,000	1,000	1,000	1,000
Health Insurance	750	750	750	1,000	1,000
Rent (20,000 SqFt @ $5.00/SqFt/yr)	8,300	8,300	8,300	8,300	8,300
Interest on Inventory (See Equipment Detail)	4,050	4,050	4,050	6,750	6,750
Interest on Notes (See Equipment Detail)	6,789	6,789	6,789	6,789	6,789
Accounting Services	1,500	1,500	1,500	1,500	1,500
Misc.	3,000	3,000	3,000	3,000	3,000
	72,799	72,799	72,799	89,979	89,979
Net Profit	15,201	31,201	47,201	46,021	62,021

10 year mill plan

He agreed, and I went to our bank and shared our vision. While they liked the concept, they asked for us to get some additional capital as a backup for our balance sheet. Thankfully, I received some help from my friend Joe, whose company put up their balance sheet for a short time and would get paid with shares of stock, which we would purchase back. They were just what we needed, and I know we wouldn't have gotten the mill built without them. Long story short, we got the loans in place, purchased a mill from a manufacturer in Turkey, and were on our way.

Here is the whole point of this little story. Prior to this takeover, this previous company had built their business the right way. Since this change, the market has shifted. Almost all their previous employees have now left, and their culture is completely changed. The result has meant that Trinity is now the number one large-diameter structural pipe manufacturer in the US. Is the company who bought out this smaller organization still a titan in the industry? Absolutely. But they have cracked the door open for businesses like Trinity to take the next step.

My hope is that when Trinity becomes a billion-dollar company, we will act in a different manner. It's one of the reasons I am writing this book. We have to stay a Big, small company. I want our systems to evolve and grow, but I want our culture to remain the same. And just as Jack Stack was an inspiration to me, I hope I can be that same inspiration for others.

Continue to Lead from the Bottom

One of my goals is to create a business that will help future generations of Griggses to prosper and succeed. Doing so is tough. In *Perpetuating the Family Business*, John Ward notes that half of all family firms fail to make it to the next generation.[22]

---

22   John Ward, *Perpetuating the Family Business: 50 Lessons Learned from Long Lasting, Successful Families in Business* (London, UK: Palgrave Macmillan, 2004), 3.

Ward says, "When I began to take an academic interest in family-owned businesses more than twenty-five years ago, my friends and colleagues often said, 'Oh, family business. Shirtsleeves to shirtsleeves in three generations!' As a member of a business-owning family, you no doubt know the concept: The first generation creates a thriving enterprise, the second generation milks it or lives off it, and the third generation doesn't have anything left and has to start over again."[23]

One of my favorite lines from scripture says that to whom much is given, much will be required.[24] At Trinity, my family and I have been blessed with so much. And to me, the only way Trinity remains sustainable is if we remain focused on those values that have made us great.

Regardless of your leadership level in an organization, remember that your success depends on those who work on your team. The moment you lose sight of this is the moment your influence will begin to diminish.

Microsoft's CEO, Satya Nadella, says, "To me, what I have sort of come to realize, what is the most innate in all of us is that ability to be able to put ourselves in other people's shoes and see the world the way they see it. That's empathy. That's at the heart of design thinking. When we say innovation is all about meeting unmet, unarticulated needs of the marketplace, it's ultimately the unmet and articulated needs of people—and organizations that are made up of people. And you need to have deep empathy. So I would say the source of all innovation is what is the most humane quality that we all have, which is empathy."[25]

Humility is foundational. As Carmine Gallo points out, humility is critical for every business owner, leader, and entrepreneur. She notes

---

23   John Ward, *Perpetuating the Family Business: 50 Lessons Learned from Long Lasting, Successful Families in Business* (London, UK: Palgrave Macmillan, 2004), 4.

24   Luke 12:48.

25   Jason Aten, "Microsoft's CEO, Satya Nadella, Says This 1 Trait Is More Important Than Talent or Experience. It's Something Anyone Can Learn," November 13, 2021, https://apple.news/AgpaclPh1S-2aZdBQEN90wA.

the importance of following what she calls the three Ls: listen to feedback, learn it all, lead with humility.[26]

To Those Afraid to Take the Leap

As you have read through this book, it's possible you might find yourself fearful for the future—afraid to take a leap into the great unknown.

If you have a family that depends on you for support, this step can be frightening. For me, I knew I would never be outworked. That could not and would not happen. So this lifestyle gave me an instant advantage over other people. If you do not have this commitment, you need to be honest with yourself.

All along my journey, I have had doubters—people who said there was no way I could make it to the next level. But these individuals only motivated me to prove them wrong. I do not spend much energy focused on what others think of me, and I root for others to succeed. I'm happy when others prosper and am grateful to be in their orbit—maybe some of their success will rub off on me!

It's not a perfect science, but to take the leap and put these principles into action, you need to start by having the right perspective. You need to be willing to put in the time, work hard, remain humble, and take risks. No, it's not always easy, but the rewards are well worth the effort.

---

26   Carmine Gallo, "The Surprising Personality Trait That Investors Admire in Entrepreneurs," November 12, 2021, https://apple.news/Azy3I7Rx4ScCQVFJ5OUnPZQ.

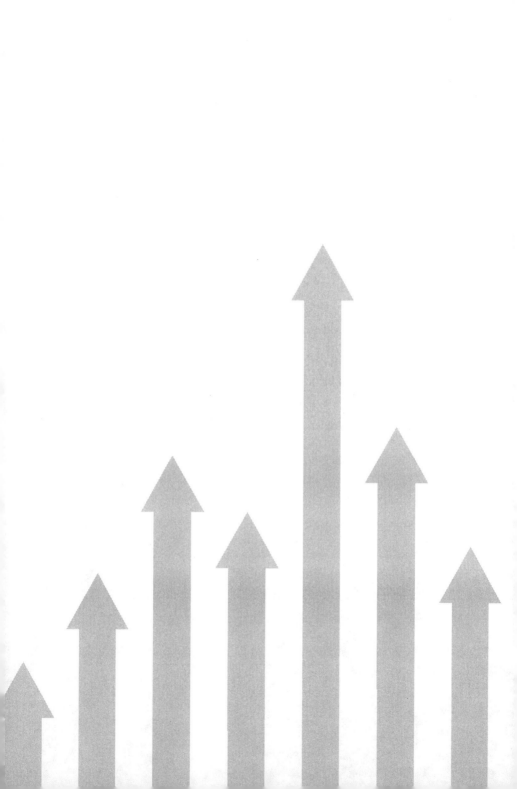

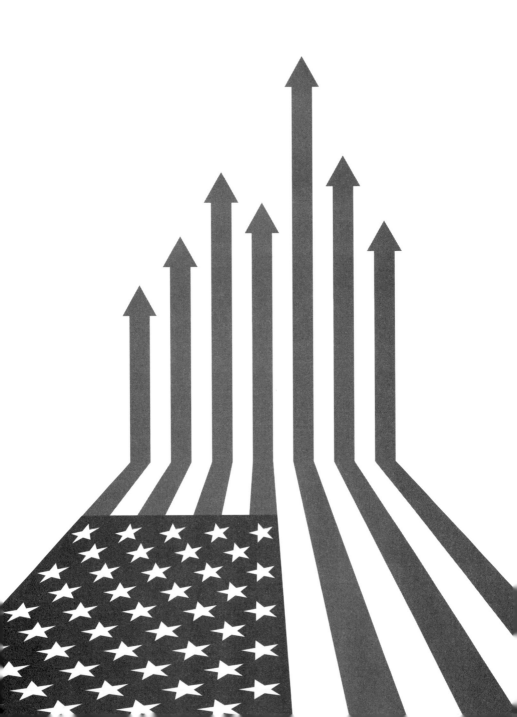

CONCLUSION

This journey of writing my life's story and the history of my business has made me go back in time and relive some of those moments in life I thought I'd forgotten. As I have done this, several points have stood out. Ones I wish hadn't taken me twenty to twenty-five years to figure out. Here are just a few of them.

First, never deal with negative people. Get them out of your life as quickly as possible! Nothing good will come from them. Life and work are hard enough without the constant drain of doubters and dissenters. Instead, focus your energy on the keepers.

Second, look for people who are smart and humble. Model humility by remembering you do not know everything and you need a strong team around you.

Third, be kind. Put yourself in other people's shoes and ask yourself how they have arrived at their conclusions. What makes them tick? Why do they act the way they do? Seek to walk a mile in their shoes before casting judgment.

Fourth, never lie and make it a requirement that everyone on your team tells the truth. You can fix mistakes, but you cannot fix lies. This sets a positive tone for your organization.

Fifth, lead well and set a good example. Remember that people will follow you and stay with you only if you are someone worth following. Remember that old phrase I've adapted: "Good and great attracts good and great." Lead yourself well and you will be surprised at the pool of talent that develops around you. The more you give, the more you receive.

Sixth, give more than you get. It's easy to want to get back at others who have wronged you. But if you take the high road in tough situations and err on the side of giving more, you will stay above the fray and keep from getting distracted.

Seventh, remember it's not about you. It's always about others. Check your ego at the door. Your team will know if you think too highly of yourself, and they will begin to check out. But if they see you as someone who has their best interests in mind, they will follow you through some pretty tough valleys.

These are just a few of the points I wished I had learned earlier. And I promise if you put the principles of this book into practice, you will be a success. It might take longer than you imagined. It took me forty years to grasp some of these ideas, but if you apply the principles we have discussed in this book, you can speed up the journey and put it into warp drive. You will inevitably encounter setbacks that knock you off your feet. But keep going.

I think the most noble thing in life is to teach people how to get better every day.

Lead from the bottom. Practice open-book leadership, always seek to improve yourself and your team, and do whatever you can to share the profits with those who work with you every day. Give your people the tools they need to thrive. Personally, I think the most noble thing in life is to teach people how to get better every day. That is the tool that keeps on giving and will change their lives.

I hope you have enjoyed all the stories of the last forty-two years of my life and that these stories and principles will help you get to your goals easier and quicker! We all stand on the shoulders of those who have stood before us. And it's my hope that this book will help you stand a little higher than I am today.

Takeaways

➡ Think of ways to grow your business right now and list them. What's stopping you from working every day to achieve those goals?

➡ Have you joined any trade associations or CEO groups? If not, why?

➡ Would you bring anyone in your family into your business? If so, how?

➡ Work to make your business a "must" place to be.

➡ Start engaging your employees *today.*

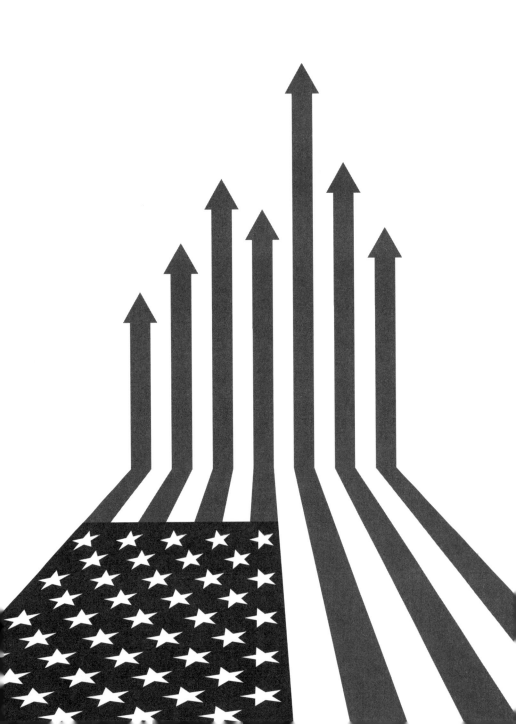

ACKNOWLEDGMENTS

As I sit here today and think about the last forty-plus years of Trinity, there are so many people to thank! Not everyone along the way who took interest in me and helped could possibly be mentioned, but a lot of you had a huge hand in helping to build what's become a real world-class company and culture.

But first and foremost comes my beautiful wife, Shelly, who has been with me every step of the way! She had to listen to me always talking about people and my situations because she was the only one who really cared a lot of times and was incredibly patient. I love you more today than ever and we're going to have a crazy journey traveling and having fun in retirement!

Secondly come the boys, who have done everything right coming into a situation of a very hard industry and a family business. Most family businesses don't survive over two generations but—AJ and Bo, boys—I am so proud of you; you can't imagine how much fun it's been working with you both every day and watching what great men you've become. Love you!

Right there with them are my two daughters-in-law, Jill and Amanda (AC)—as Shelly says, the Griggs family has been blessed with two wonderful daughters!

And finally my grandkids, the blessing of my life: Parker, Avery, and Roman! I love you all so much (plus, let's hope there are more to come!).

Now to my Trinity family! Sal, my first partner, I wouldn't have made it without you; thanks for your hard-nosed love. Phyllis, our first employee, I couldn't have done it without you! Vince, my second partner, you got us through some tough spots, so thank you.

Now the Trinity leaders we've helped to build: Kristy Pride—you've taken every job thrown at you and killed it; Bryan Davis, my little brother, who walked in the door as a young smart kid and is now taking over in my seat—you deserve it!

Jim Nazzoli, who built our accounting department and took on the job of chief improvement officer—even though you didn't like the title—I think you like your current title better: COO!

Jason Perry, who has grown with us and is now our CFO: thank you. I never have to worry about the numbers, good or bad, though I still just wish you'd give me a guess sometimes.

All the guys in the shop—early ones are Kent Allen, Al Gray, Bill Jaggie; then Paul, Drew, and Evan ... you all are real leaders. Thanks for what you've accomplished. You are KILLING it!

Sorry if I missed anyone. I'm here to say I love you and I know you'll get to $1 billion in sales; the why is the people and the how is in this book!

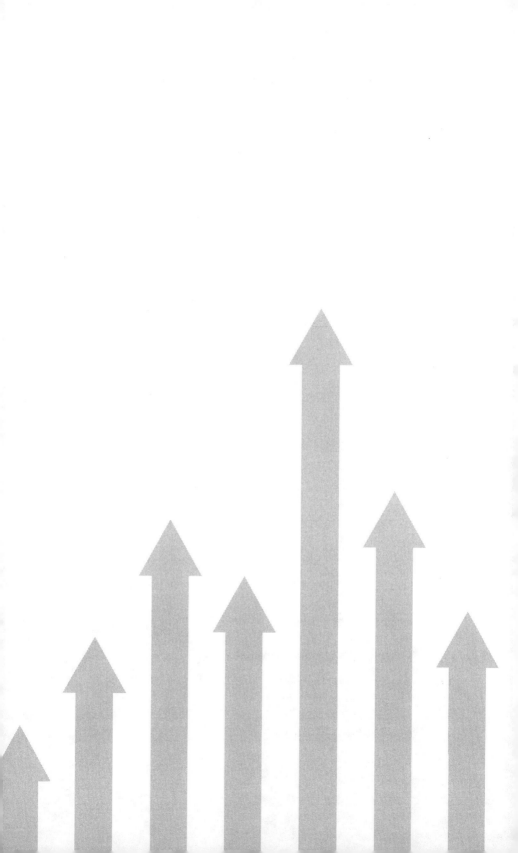

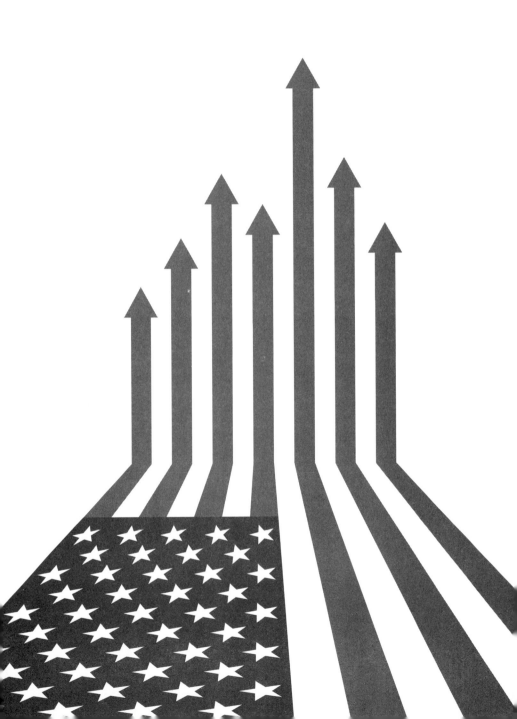

ABOUT THE AUTHOR

A lifelong Missourian, Robert Griggs graduated from the University of Missouri, Columbia in 1977. In 1979, Robert did something his college friends found daring—bordering on crazy: he and a business associate started their own company, Trinity Products, Inc. While his contemporaries struggled in entry-level corporate jobs, the twenty-three-year-old agricultural economics major from rural Missouri saw opportunity in the steel pipe business, and grabbed it. Initially, Trinity Products' mission was to provide quality products and services to the construction industry, piling contractors, road-boring contractors, utility contractors, and the caisson industry.

Then in 1986, Griggs secured a lease on fifteen acres of property and built a fabrication facility. Adding fabrication services increased the value the company could offer its existing customers, as well as further diversify its customer base. This expansion brought about the addition of high-rise sign structures, which led to the addition of billboard fabrication and other more complicated fabrication. The result? Trinity set itself apart from its competition.

By the early 1990s, Griggs saw an even brighter future ahead for the steel industry, and aspired to take Trinity to new heights. He bought out his partner, and by 1999, he had begun expanding the company's operation by building a new $1.3 million facility that included a thirty-thousand-square-foot fabrication shop. The addition of a CNC multitorch burning table to custom cut parts from plate significantly increased Trinity's fabrication capabilities. Two years later, Griggs added new equipment for cutting angles, channels, and beams to facilitate the growing billboard and cell tower divisions. Responding to his customers' specific needs and to facilitate increased production requirements, Griggs added a ten-thousand-square-foot coating facility and a CNC beam liner to Trinity's fabrication capabilities by midsummer of 2002.

In 2004, Griggs broke ground for his most ambitious expansion project to date, a $15 million spiral-welded pipe mill. The move was a gamble. Only one other facility of its kind existed, and the market for spiral-welded pipe was still unproven. Griggs's enduring goal was to be the only totally vertically integrated supplier in the steel industry. The company has enjoyed a 127 percent growth in sales each year. Annual sales have grown from $2.1 million in 1993 to projected sales of $300 million in 2022.

Griggs applies his out-of-the-box thinking to his business as well as the management of his company. In 1995, Trinity became one of the first companies of its size to move to open-book management, a management format that encourages employees to become involved in the decision-making process directly related to their job. At the time, Griggs's deep-seated belief was that he could not grow Trinity's sales, profitability, and culture on his own. To become truly profitable, he and his management team needed to become "teachers" of business. Since he viewed his employees as "experts" in their respective fields, workers were encouraged to voice their input and were rewarded when the contribution was effective. Today, everyone—from shop and office personnel to management—understands Trinity's income statement. The company shares financial information at regular monthly finance meetings and solicits input from employees on current issues. Benchmarks are established and goals are set collectively. As their objectives are reached, all employees share in the profits. In 2001, Griggs was honored by the state of Missouri with the Governor's Achievement Award for Economic Development and the 2001 Innovative Training/Workforce Development Award.

Griggs has also served as president and treasurer of the National Association of Steel Pipe Distributors (NASPD), an international organization of more than two hundred steel distributors. He has spent his entire career in the steel and fabrications industry. Griggs bought out his original partner in 1993. Since that time, Trinity's revenues have grown from $2.2 million to $300 million in 2022. Projections for sales in 2014 are $70 million.

There are two overriding themes when it comes to Robert Griggs: 1) don't tell a lie, and 2) the more you give, the more you get. Don't tell a lie is pretty simple, as it is about the only thing you can do at Trinity that will get you fired. The more you give, the more you get is slightly more complicated. Griggs believes that when you make someone else's life better, your life will be better as a result. This is not just a monetary thing either. Griggs makes it a point to learn about and know the families of all the employees as well as what is important to them. He will then make every attempt to help that person achieve those goals. He encourages all employees to think in this fashion as well. Each year Trinity supports one of the local food pantries with a "canned food drive" as a way of giving back to the community. With management having this mindset, employees generally feel like they are part of something and want to come to work. They look at this as more than just a job, and as such, Trinity has seen a reduction of turnover throughout the company.

Along with his wife, Griggs currently lives in St. Charles, Missouri. His two sons are also both University of Missouri, Columbia graduates and are currently working for Trinity Products.

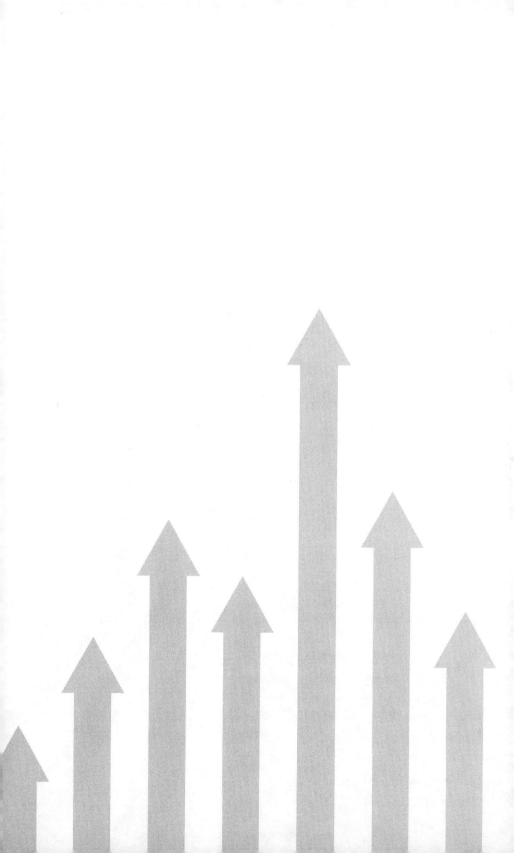

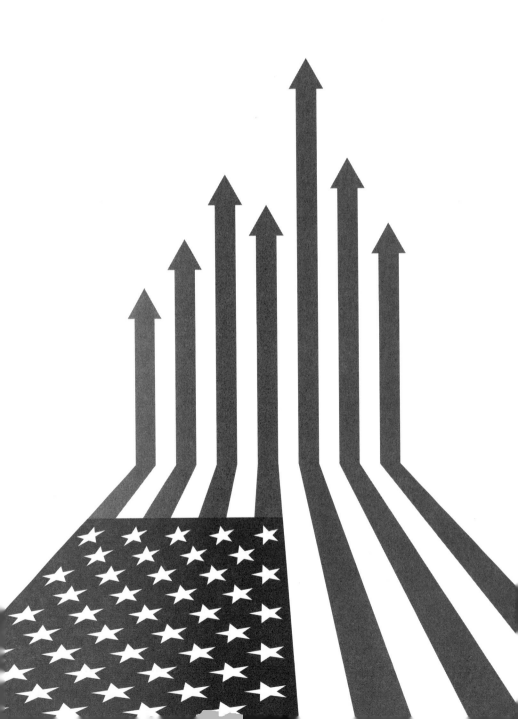

PERSONAL TESTIMONIALS

After completing this book, I contacted several people at Trinity and asked them to share their unvarnished perspectives. How had the principles outlined in this book impacted their lives? Here are the responses I received.

Ryan Hoffman, Purchasing Manager, Fifteen Years

What attracted you to Trinity in the first place?

My situation was a bit unique. I was furloughed from US Steel but was still receiving compensation from them when I applied with Trinity. A friend of mine who was employed by Trinity recommended I at least submit my résumé, seeing as my background was within steel production and Trinity had just started a new pipe mill. I was growing concerned that my furloughed compensation package was going to expire prior to being called back to work with US Steel. My wife and I were planning to start a family, and I didn't feel comfortable doing so with my career in a state of flux. So I accepted a position with Trinity after interviewing, and an offer was proposed.

How has your time at Trinity changed the way you view concepts such as open-book leadership, continuous improvement, and ESOPs?

I came from a huge conglomerate where one would barely communicate with anyone outside the department they operated within. So the concept of open-book management and inclusion was a foreign concept to me. At first, I didn't understand why Robert would choose to share the financials with everyone, because reading financial statements (income, balance sheets) isn't a skill that everyone possesses. At the time, I thought it would confuse some folks and leave them with a false sense of how much money the company nets. What I didn't realize is how well opening up the financials would encourage folks to get involved in managing even the smallest of expenses. And managing those expenses was their way of affecting the profits we would all share. I was honestly blown away at the interest level ranging from the top salesperson to the janitor when it came to doing what they could to improve processes, reduce expenses, and maximize profits.

What would be one piece of advice you would share with "middle managers" who would like to incorporate these concepts and change the way they lead their teams?

Be inclusive. Ask questions about how you as their superior can make them love their jobs and want to show up every day.

Buddy Sumpter, Sales Manager, Nine Years

What attracted you to Trinity in the first place?

For me, the driving factor in joining Trinity was my desire to continue to work for a steel pipe manufacturer that believed in supporting the local economy as well as the US economy! I knew Robert long before he had a pipe mill and was honored when he asked me to come work for him and Trinity Products.

How has your time at Trinity changed the way you view concepts such as open-book leadership, continuous improvement, and ESOPs?

In my other jobs, I had never worked for a company that used open-book management/leadership or continuous improvement principles. Trinity is also the first company that I've worked for that is an ESOP. While open-book management and continuous improvement principles have clearly helped Trinity evolve into the successful company it is, the MOST important factor has been Robert's passion in EVERY aspect of running the business! His energy and spirit is unmatched and, quite frankly, unbelievable. His enthusiasm is contagious, and you can't help but be "all in" when you hear Robert talk about his next idea. The way Robert has led Trinity and the passion he showed in every detail of running the company is what will make Trinity a successful ESOP.

*What would be one piece of advice you
would share with "middle managers" who
would like to incorporate these concepts and
change the way they lead their teams?*

I believe all of management, as well as the other employees, will benefit
from Robert's example as the new "owners" of Trinity Products. The
principle of "always get better" will keep the company moving forward
and prospering!

Bryan Davis, Vice President of Sales, Twenty Years

What attracted you to Trinity in the first place?

Being old school, I was looking for a J.O.B. in 2001 and answered a
newspaper ad. I certainly didn't envision a career at that point.

*How has your time at Trinity changed the way
you view concepts such as open-book leadership,
continuous improvement, and ESOPs?*

Over the years of helping to implement open-book leadership, I truly
believe this is the only way companies should be managed. The group
is stronger than the individual, and both of these concepts emphasize
the group. The final move to make in that evolution is the ESOP, and
that is going to positively impact many families in ways they don't
even comprehend yet.

*What would be one piece of advice you
would share with "middle managers" who*

would like to incorporate these concepts and change the way they lead their teams?

One piece of advice for folks wanting to implement these concepts is not to overly complicate things. Don't confuse simple with easy. To do this properly is quite simple but is hard work. Do the work, because it is both liberating and rewarding in ways that you can't imagine until it has happened. Celebrate your successes and learn from everything else. Failure only happens when you quit. DON'T QUIT!

Phyllis MacConnell, Special Projects Coordinator, Forty-Two Years

What attracted you to Trinity in the first place?

I came to Trinity five months after they incorporated in 1979. I graduated from high school, needed to work, applied, and got hired at Associated Pipe, where Robert was a sales rep. They liked my work ethic, and so when they walked across the parking lot and rented an office space to start Trinity, they asked for me to hang on, and when they could afford to pay me, they would give me a call to come work for them. And so here I am forty-two years later.

How has your time at Trinity changed the way you view concepts such as open-book leadership, continuous improvement, and ESOPs?

I believe because of these concepts and sharing financials, being open to all about the business and the money we are actually making or not making, and talking about our company strategy and goals has helped us remain like a family even as we continued to grow and add employees. I think that it makes folks feel included and a part of the business no matter what their job is here.

What would be one piece of advice you would share with "middle managers" who would like to incorporate these concepts and change the way they lead their teams?

Ask their people regularly how they are doing. If they need anything, thank them for their work. As an employee it means a lot to be asked how you are doing, to know that your manager/supervisor knows your name, recognizes what you do and if you are doing a good job. It means a lot for folks to hear that. I think sometimes in life it's the people who are not doing the right thing that tend to get the attention, and the ones showing up on time and doing it right sort of go unnoticed. Since I have been working for Robert, every day he arrives to work at each facility, he first drives to the shops and talks to the production folks, asks them how they are doing, and tries to get to know them. He does that to the folks on the sales floor as well. Just last week, I was looking out the office window and saw his truck driving around the pipe yard early in the morning … forty-two years later!

Jeff Nuernberger, Sales, Thirteen Years

What attracted you to Trinity in the first place?

I had been in sales for approximately ten years prior to joining Trinity Products, and of all the different sales jobs I've held, most with big, national corporations, I never felt like I was part of a team where the results I produced made much of a difference. I saw an opportunity to come to Trinity and work with a group of professionals whose daily efforts have an immediate impact on the success and growth of the company.

How has your time at Trinity changed the way you view concepts such as open-book leadership, continuous improvement, and ESOPs?

Prior to starting at Trinity, I was not familiar with these concepts, as it simply was not something that I experienced in "Corporate America." I believe that a company's success is driven by the employees, and when you have programs like these in place, it serves as a vital tool in hiring and retaining the best people. Who wouldn't want to work for a company that shares all the financial info and allows you to be part of a team constantly looking for ways to get better, and on top of that, be part owner?

What would be one piece of advice you would share with "middle managers" who would like to incorporate these concepts and change the way they lead their teams?

The one piece of advice I would recommend is to include everyone on their team and encourage participation. Do a good job of explaining the goals of the company and the desired outcomes and benefits. Get everyone steering the ship in the same direction.

Kevin Henry, QA/QC Manager, Fifteen Years

What attracted you to Trinity in the first place?

Me being hired was a stroke of GOOD LUCK in my eyes for me. The first time I attempted I was turned away. About four or five months later I received a call from an employee who said Trinity was looking for a fabrications guy. I gave it another shot but had to prove what I knew. After my initial hire I was tried at practically every position in the shop with success, which lasted five or six years. Robert approached me with an opportunity to start his quality department, and I could move back to the shop if it didn't work for me. Nine years later I'm still with him as his manager in the quality department. Thank you, sir!

How has your time at Trinity changed the way you view concepts such as open-book leadership, continuous improvement, and ESOPs?

I have found that with the way Robert has run the company (open-book leadership, continuous improvement, and ESOPs) since I came on is in most ways how I would run my own. Honesty, loyalty, and a sense of learning as much as you can possibly retain/handle. You have a voice, and knowing that makes you feel like you're a part of something HUGE and important. A certain type of family environment. Wouldn't change any of it!

What would be one piece of advice you would share with "middle managers" who

would like to incorporate these concepts and change the way they lead their teams?

My advice to other managers would be to let their guys speak and have a certain say in how they do their jobs. I mean, after all, we don't know everything that needs to be known. Don't be closed minded or have objections to doing what got us in the positions we are in currently. Jump in and assist if necessary. I have found that there is a maximum amount of respect that is earned if they know you're not afraid of getting DIRTY alongside them!!!

Justin Herren, Business Development, Ten Years

What attracted you to Trinity in the first place?

I had an existing relationship with Trinity for a few years before becoming an employee. Trinity was one of our vendors at my previous employer, and I had heard great things about the transparency between management and the sales group, which I would later learn was directly associated with Trinity's open-book management program. When the opportunity presented itself to apply for a sales position, I took it!

How has your time at Trinity changed the way you view concepts such as open-book leadership, continuous improvement, and ESOPs?

Throughout my ten-year tenure at Trinity, I have been blessed to experience and benefit from Trinity's phenomenal growth, and that's directly attributed to open-book leadership, the continuous improvement program, and more recently the transition to being

100 percent employee owned. I have personally witnessed an overall greater engagement from fellow employees because we knew that our opinions and ideas were not only considered, but they were sought after and implemented. That process created the foundation for true teamwork, and the fruits of that labor have certainly been enjoyed by all. And now that we're all owners of Trinity through the ESOP, the meaning of *team* has been taken to a new level!

What would be one piece of advice you would share with "middle managers" who would like to incorporate these concepts and change the way they lead their teams?

If I could offer any advice to managers wishing to incorporate these concepts, it would be to actively and earnestly seek out the engagement of your team! They have a wide range of life experiences and acquired knowledge to share. Collectively you can accomplish more than any single leader or manager could ever do.

Adam Manz, Sales, Four Years

What attracted you to Trinity in the first place?

After doing my summer internship at Trinity, the main thing that made me want to join after college was the atmosphere of growth taking place. I knew Trinity was a smaller private business doing big projects in the industry, but the number of ideas to grow the company further and develop new product lines are what made me want to stick around for the ride. It taught me that you can't truly see a company for what it is until you sit down with the people running it and see what their vision is for the future.

How has your time at Trinity changed the way you view concepts such as open-book leadership, continuous improvement, and ESOPs?

Being there to see important functions on how Trinity is run made me feel more incorporated with Trinity. Open-book leadership does a lot to show an employee what it takes to make a profit and how that affects the company overall. The involvement I've had in continuous improvement meetings boosted my self-confidence and gave me the opportunity to think critically about what can be done to make Trinity grow efficiently. Having the company change gears to an ESOP style of business topped off the feeling of incorporation because it provides a physical notion of sharing growth and allows a greater appreciation in witnessing the financials through open-book management. All together this creates an employee who experiences a sense of ownership and respect for their role at Trinity.

What would be one piece of advice you would share with "middle managers" who would like to incorporate these concepts and change the way they lead their teams?

The one piece of advice I would share is for middle managers to actively create an environment where their employees feel connected to the bottom line of the company. Make sure they know every dollar made in revenue and profit is a direct result of their daily efforts in keeping the company running and working together as a team. Once they have that, do something to allow a percentage of profits to be shared with the employees so there is a greater incentive to create ways to improve profits, decrease costs, and overall work with an ownership mindset.

Evan Hauer, Mill Plant Manager, Ten Years

How would you encourage others to implement open-book leadership?

Regarding your first question, you hit the nail on the head for me. It starts with ME implementing the processes in my daily routine and imparting those values to my team. "Start with yourself. Lead yourself well by doing little things with excellence. And as you do this, impart these values to your team."

How important are relationships?

I feel relationships are also the keys that take us where we want to go. No one gets to where they want to be on their own. If I were to start somewhere else, I would start by fostering good, honest relationships with subordinates, peers, and superiors. People must trust and respect you if you are going to enact any significant change. Once people trust in you and see the benefits of how you conduct yourself, then you gain their "buy-in" to what you are trying to achieve.

Why is buy-in so important?

When you have a person's or team's buy-in then you can really set standards and processes that people will follow. As you set quality standards for yourself, your team, and processes, it is hard for anyone who takes pride in what they do not to notice the benefits. If it makes sense, then it makes dollars, as they say, and for most people dollars equal recognition for individual efforts, improved working conditions and processes, sense of accomplishment, and increased company profits—which leads to higher earning potential and quality of life for the individual. All of this continues to create even more buy-in, which is the key.

Where should people start?

I would start with small team projects that immediately relieve daily frustration in some process. An example would be designing welding fixtures that are easier to set up and adjust during production. When the team sees the benefits from small projects and the sense of accomplishment it brings, I generally find they are fueled to find the next improvement they can make. Inevitably management will take notice of the fruits of the process and want to implement at a higher level. The hardest part of the process for me used to be failing. But it is important to see failures as a lead into the next fruitful solution and to encourage your team that failing is not just OK but at times a good thing. Failing helps us find the best solutions.

How important is continuous improvement?

I think CI is imperative to survival and is another way of innovating. If a company cannot innovate or continue to improve, then they most likely will not flourish.

Rich Adams, Head of Production, Six Years

Why is team development so important?

Team development is paramount. Regardless of the *task* developmental process (training employees to do the manager's skills so that the manager can promote), a highly functional team is the foundation of any successful improvement initiative. A manager in this role should focus on developing trust, a fearlessness of communication, and the ability to absorb criticism without impacting ego. With these three items in place, task training becomes organic and far easier to do.

This comes from, for me personally, a position of humility in regard to the treatment of that team. The manager working to implement must see themselves fully in service to the people who work for them, setting aside ambition and bias for the betterment of the whole. This facilitates an honesty and *appropriate* vulnerability that provides the example for the remainder of the team to follow. This should not be confused with being "soft" or "unfocused," but is a humanistic way to leverage strong relationships without sacrificing the importance of a leadership hierarchy.

How do you approach execution?

The manager should focus to develop a clear understanding of what they CAN control. Know the rules of the game and stay within those rules, especially early. The lack of authority to make immediate change can be so overwhelmingly frustrating that they may lose sight of the places where they do have that ability, causing failure before they even started. It is vital to dial in on the things they can do as a focal point for their end goal and wash away the things that are solely out of your hands.

Few things grease the wheels of change like positive results. Large-scale change will only come with objective results. You will need to bring evidence of them to produce the larger change you desire.

Paul Wilkerson, Maintenance Manager, Fourteen Years

Why is buy-in important?

If you don't have the buy-in and engagement, then it won't be successful. People want to feel engaged; they want to feel like their opinions matter, and they love to see their ideas or thoughts get put into action. This is something Trinity has done very well in my opinion with the COSI teams and Post-it Notes, etc.

On the flip side, the worst thing you can do is encourage ideas and creativity and then not act on it. Sometimes money doesn't allow for a great idea, but I've seen items on a list for years until we were able to make it happen, or we were able to make a compromise somewhere.

How do you brainstorm and come up with fresh ideas?

This part for me is always a lot of fun—gathering people in a room and having them throw out ideas and have discussions on those ideas. This is where the Post-it Notes come into play, but a simple list in an Excel sheet has been our method for so many years and it has worked well.

It's amazing what people have already thought about when it comes to making their job more efficient and better. *If we did this, it would save us X, or if we did this it would speed this up by X.*

What is the importance of staying focused on ROI?

Once you have your list, start looking at the ROI on each item. Have the team members do this so that there's more engagement and buy-in. This also gives them more awareness on what things cost and how hard it is to implement some ideas.

How do you plan?

Sort the list from biggest ROI or lowest-hanging fruit and start planning how to make it happen! Break the list up into teams and assign projects and tasks to individuals. This will encourage growth and engagement. Don't let all the tasks fall on any one particular person. That person will burn out and the tasks will not happen, or they will get dragged out. If you do have teams and team leaders, make sure to train the team leaders on how to delegate. Delegation is hard for some people, and they end up just "doing everything themselves" and get frustrated or fail.

How do you execute?

Once you have the plan, make it happen, have weekly meetings on it, and ask for updates. Don't get mad if progress isn't made. People have full-time jobs along with working on these tasks. Once it's on the list, it doesn't come off unless it's complete or no longer becomes a need. Celebrate the successes!

How do you track and follow up?

Once projects are complete, make sure to follow up with them over time to see how they are going and if they are still being implemented. Too many times I've seen something completed, and then a year later you find out that they only used something for three months and then stopped because of X and didn't tell anyone.

Darla Ratliff, Staff Accountant, Fourteen Years

What attracted you to Trinity in the first place?

Truthfully, what attracted me to join Trinity fourteen years ago was it being another pipe company close to home and not a big corporation. Yes, accounting is pretty much the same no matter where you go, but learning a business's lingo and products are not. Since I've been here, I've come to value the family atmosphere.

How has your time at Trinity changed the way you view concepts such as open-book leadership, continuous improvement, and ESOPs?

Before I came to Trinity, I didn't know about open-book management. Now that I've lived it, I can't imagine being in a company where it's not practiced. I feel doing this prepared us as employees to be owners in the ESOP because we started caring about expenses off the start.

Implementing COSI several years ago, I feel, was one of the best things we could've done. If a company is going to stay afloat in today's world, they need to be open to change that will improve the company as a whole. This keeps the company running like a well-oiled machine instead of limping along.

What would be one piece of advice you would share with "middle managers" who would like to incorporate these concepts and change the way they lead their teams?

My advice is to be patient and make sure everyone understands the company's financials even if they need to give classes as a group or individually. I noticed through the years, the more everyone understood, the better our finance meetings were … even if it wasn't the best news, because they understood why.

Kristy Pride, Special Projects Coordinator, Over Twenty Years

What attracted you to Trinity in the first place?

Why would I want to work in a double-wide trailer next to a dirty quarry along the river in Missouri when I came from a financial services company in a skyscraper in Dallas? ENERGY and can-do attitude. I wanted to be part of a team where everyone's voice was heard, problems were worked through together, and taking care of family was always the priority. While the path has been sometimes unexpected, the journey has never been boring.

How has your time at Trinity changed the way you view concepts such as open-book leadership, continuous improvement, and ESOPs?

All choices have consequences. Good choices generally have better consequences. How can anyone make good choices without good information? Open-book leadership reinforces the idea that accurate information should be shared with all levels of the organization. Bad choices by anyone in a group—from the floor sweeper to the president—will have negative effects on all. Fostering open sharing of information also removes hiding places for problems and people who are not going to improve the company going forward.

What would be one piece of advice you would share with "middle managers" who would like to incorporate these concepts and change the way they lead their teams?

Always tell the truth. Problems can always be solved, but lies can never be fixed.

Kevin Comiskey, Director of Business Development, Two Years

What attracted you to Trinity in the first place?

The main reason I joined Trinity is that I trusted the people I was going to work with at Trinity. In a very short window at a previous place, I lost all of the trust I had for my superiors, and it was impossible to do great things when there is no trust. Trinity was up front and honest since the beginning; there was no situation where I was just being told what I wanted to hear. I hate when someone does not have the guts to give you the hard answer, and that's what I was leaving in my past employer.

How has your time at Trinity changed the way you view concepts such as open-book leadership, continuous improvement, and ESOPs?

Open-book leadership has been eye opening in a good way. It makes you realize that what you do affects everyone, not just yourself.

ESOP is a concept that I was completely naive to when I first came over, but the more I look into it, the more it makes you proud to be an owner with everyone. It gives everyone a piece of the pie, not just the guys in the corner offices. Continuous improvement has been the easiest thing for me; I am way more involved in every piece of the business now. Previously I only needed to figure out how to sell the product; I never worried about the warehouse, the office, the admin employees, purchasing, inventory turns, average cost, IT, etc., etc. It has been a very rewarding challenge up to this point.

What would be one piece of advice you would share with "middle managers" who would like to incorporate these concepts and change the way they lead their teams?

The most important thing about managing people is the term KYP—know your personnel. If you do not know the strengths and weaknesses of your employees, then you are constantly going to be asking the person to do things they are not good at; therefore, they will constantly be letting you down. You can't fit a round peg in a square hole. The main things you need to look for are these three things:

1. Work ethic: Can't teach it and you typically can't change it. Either they have it or they don't.

2. Self-awareness: The person needs to know their strengths and weaknesses; if they try to be something they are not, then it will be difficult for you to figure out their potential.

3. Good attitude: You can't have someone who has a bad attitude; they will bring the rest of the team down with a bad attitude.

In the short amount of time I have spent at Trinity, I feel like most of the company fits these three qualities, and I guess that goes back to the first question, "Why did I come to Trinity?"

Chad Duffin, Vice President Sales, Distribution Division, Two Years

What attracted you to Trinity in the first place?

My attraction to Trinity Products came from multiple personal experiences. Prior to coming on board at Trinity Products, I worked for twenty years with my previous employer. Throughout that twenty-year experience, I observed money and success change people. Those who were once driven by work ethic, morality, and a desire to make others great slowly morphed into entitled individuals who lost sight of the value of the team. These individuals were executives receiving incomes in the 1 percent category. They should have valued the reality that appreciating others ultimately leads to their own personal success, and without those people they would have nothing. However, with every year that passed, so did their appreciation. Before you knew it, half the team that built the company had departed.

One of the other reasons for my interest in Trinity was my personal experience with Trinity Products. Our previous company supplied and serviced Trinity for many years. Throughout those years, I was able to better understand Trinity and what made them successful. Conversations with leadership often led to their praise of not only their employees but our employees as well.

Trinity was—and still is—a humble organization that takes pride in their employees' personal and professional success. In addition I was fortunate enough to experience adversity with Robert Griggs and Bryan Davis prior to joining Trinity. For me, adversity is important, as life is simple when things are going well. It is through adversity that you learn everything you need to know about someone.

During COVID-19, numerous companies had projects and contracts canceled. Trinity was no different, but the manner in which they handled the situation was. Robert and Bryan both made personal calls to me openly and honestly talking through the situation. They offered detailed plans on how they were going to handle the surplus supply as well as the delayed payables. Most importantly, they communicated and did not shy away from the situation. Through this adversity came great clarity for me. A clarity that later drew me to going into business with Trinity Products.

Finally, my father was the main factor in working at Trinity Products. At the time, we had two other private investment groups who were inquiring in our team. A big influence for me came from my father's philosophy to always surround yourself with others who genuinely put others first. This was not only proven through many conversations; it was also proven through ESOP programs, profit sharing bonuses, and the pride with which numerous employees spoke of Trinity Products.

How has your time at Trinity changed the way you view concepts such as open-book leadership, continuous improvement, and ESOPs?

I am a bit embarrassed to admit this, but this topic is a work in progress for me. Inherently, I am an individual who trusts others to a fault. I was raised this way and live my personal life this way. Through some of my previous business experiences, I have been tainted a bit. That said, Trinity's open-book leadership style is bringing my business trust more in line with my personal trust style. The ESOP program has a big influence on me and how I view Trinity Products. I am very motivated to maximize company value. It would be a dream to sit at a company picnic with a Trinity warehouse veteran of twenty years who is retiring with $100,000 plus in their ESOP. I would not say these programs have changed my opinion on how strongly I feel about open-book management, as this has always been my style. That said, these styles were never celebrated in my previous life. Thus, I would say these concepts have reinstilled my faith that people who put others first are still out there.

What would be one piece of advice you would share with "middle managers" who would like to incorporate these concepts and change the way they lead their teams?

People want to be a part of something great. Celebrate the reality that all employees are owners. Empower them to make decisions as an owner and not an individual. You cannot adapt an open-book policy and then judge employees for their ideas. Do not put square pegs in round holes. People thrive working on pieces of business within their expertise.

Finally, you have to understand that your biggest challenges will come from employees who are not self-aware. You have to commit to putting people only in situations where their talents meet their responsibilities.

Notes